I0434304

Relationship Maintenance and Repair Manual

Relationship Maintenance and Repair Manual

Harold D. Renshaw

Writers Club Press
San Jose New York Lincoln Shanghai

Relationship Maintenance and Repair Manual

All Rights Reserved © 2002 by Harold D. Renshaw

No part of this book may be reproduced or transmitted in any form or by any means, graphic, electronic, or mechanical, including photocopying, recording, taping, or by any information storage retrieval system, without the permission in writing from the publisher.

Writers Club Press
an imprint of iUniverse, Inc.

For information address:
iUniverse, Inc.
5220 S. 16th St., Suite 200
Lincoln, NE 68512
www.iuniverse.com

Not a substitute for therapy in extreme cases.

ISBN: 0-595-22793-7

Printed in the United States of America

To wives and husbands and especially my wife, Betty.

Contents

Preface

My wife and I were checking out at the supermarket one day when a woman rushed up to me and hugged me. "I love this guy!" she announced to my embarrassment. Then, as quickly as she had come she left but she called back over her shoulder, "You better write that book!"

It was then that I realized who she was. She and her husband were a couple I had counseled a year before. I had told them that I wanted to write a book about marriage and they had encouraged me to do that and Marge got in this last reminder in the supermarket.

I believe that we all have a story or a bit of wisdom to pass on and we should do it. After more years than I care to count I have been taught a few things about human beings and their relationships and problems. My teachers have included a handful from my college and graduate education and more than I can count from clients I have met.

Clients have often asked if I was considering writing an article or a book because they would sure like to have a copy if I did. The vanity of having my thoughts in print along with this flattering encouragement of my clients combined with a sense of obligation I felt to share something of what I had learned finally squeezed my brain enough to put together this book.

To be honest, I feel a spiritual obligation to share what I believe is a gift from God. He didn't give me all of that education and all of those tremendous experiences with my clients for my use only or to "keep under a bushel," as the Book says. I have to drain everything I have found useful out of my head and heart and lay it out there for you.

As I wrote I imagined you, my reader and in my imagination you sometimes spoke up and said, "But what about this problem?" In response, I would revise. Sometimes you would say, "That doesn't make sense!" and I would re-examine that chapter and more often than not, you were right. I thank you for that.

You also told me to keep some humor in this work. I tried. But I also added some of my cartoons about a dysfunctional couple, Edna and Quincy Eener, who were inspired by some of mistakes in attitude and actions of a few of my clients.

No book just pops out of a rock. Many people help create it. But as I tried to think of everyone who contributed I realized that the list is endless. I want to thank my teachers, both from the academic and professional world and especially those clients who have let me into their lives with such great trust. I especially want to thank my wife, Betty, who has encouraged me and the lady I called, "Marge," for that hug that contributed greatly to my finally getting words into my laptop.

Introduction

About Me

I just didn't get it. I didn't understand what I was getting myself into. I was scared as could be when I stood at the altar watching a beautiful woman in white, at her father's arm walking down the aisle toward me. She looked very pretty but her confidence sent a chill up my spine, because she looked like she knew what she was doing. I didn't. As she got closer I realized that this was not a dream, that the world was not going to end and God wasn't going to intervene. This was going to happen! This was real!

I knew I was entering a world I didn't understand, a mysterious world where women seemed comfortable while men can only stumble around. I didn't get it. I stumbled around trying desperately to look like I knew what I was doing but my wife knew what she was doing and I was only pretending.

When I was a kid, I saw the world divided into two parts, those who had fun and those who got married. When I was a senior in high school one of my classmates announced that he was going to get married right after graduation. All of guys were amazed. As far as any of us knew our friend had not even dated. How could he be the first one married? Didn't he want to have fun first?

That was scary. Someone who had gone to classes with us and had shared jokes and tall tales was going to leave our world and enter that very serious world where adults live. My friends and I were left in a state of shock. We avoided the issue in typical male fashion, we made sexual allusions and finally sunk down to another common level, we talked about cars.

Like soldiers in battle, we were shocked by the fall of our buddy. We knew that it was only a matter of time before our turn would come. There were matrimonial bullets out there with our names on them.

So, I went off to study to be a priest. Safe! While I was in the seminary I would be living safely away from women and I would be able to forget about that bullet. It would have to hit someone else.

But guess what? There were still women out there and worse of all, there were still women in my head. The ones out there would sometimes visit their brothers in the seminary and they would check their brothers' friends out like lionesses circling a herd of gazelles. That's where I met my future wife, the woman getting closer and closer to me as I stood at the altar. She told me later that she felt that I would someday be her husband.

And now we were standing in front of a priest at St. Peter and Paul church in Omaha and I hadn't dodged that bullet after all. I couldn't run and I couldn't do anything but just say that I would accept my fate.

The greatest question for men who stand at the edge of that abyss is something like this: "Is there life after wedding or do I just cease to exist? And if there is life, is it hell or is it heaven?"

After the wedding ceremony, my wife conducted me down the aisle and out into the sunshine. Friends and relatives congratulated us. Some of my old seminary buddies were there and they were equally congratulatory. I think I took a bullet for some of them as they went off to enjoy the bliss of the obliviously unwed.

Marriage brought on changes. Before we got married I went to Sam's Supermarket and bought $15 dollars worth of groceries. I explained to Dave, the manager, that I was getting married and I wanted to buy our first week's groceries. Dave laughed and told me that he would be meeting my new wife within a day or two of the wedding. He did. My bride taught me that while we might be able to live on love, peanut butter, bread, a large can of peaches and assorted snack foods would not sustain a household.

One of the changes that occurred was that I found myself accepted into the Oppressed Husbands Fraternity (OHF). I could sit with them, drink coffee or beer and we could listen to tales of woe and share funny stories about how dumb women are. I was still in the initiation phase and could only listen but it was like basic training. You learn to do a lot of belching and backslapping. The members of OHF—and it is a large group with international membership—hide their marital confusion and pain behind sexist language and lots of bitter humor. They talk about sexy women (other than our wives). It usually degenerates into talking about cars or sports by the end of meeting.

My wife and I started out our marriage with the same friends we had before we got married. We would visit them, go to bars, and have swimming parties and backyard philosophical discussions. Then we had a child. After that, life was very complicated. Just to go to out the door required a great deal of preparation. There were diaper bags, lotions, bottles, miscellaneosities of great variety. All of this had to be loaded into a Volkswagen Beetle. In the winter, with all of the extra blankets (my Bug only heated my left ankle) we had to dig to find the kid. All of that baggage and a child seat left no room for toting friends around from party to party.

So, I did the only thing a man could do. I took over the social obligations and left my wife and child in the comfort of our little apartment. While this seemed perfectly OK to me, for some reason it didn't seem to please my wife. We went back to toting all that stuff which had only multiplied after we acquired a second child.

Gradually, we found ourselves socializing with people in similar predicaments. They understood our limited mobility. We could play off the kids together (sometimes for minutes at a time) while wives discussed kids and husbands held OHF meetings. As the kids got older they began to demand less of our attention. My wife and I could have conversations together but we forgot what it was that we used share. We had become strangers or worse. We didn't hate each other we just sort of floated along together, familiar logs side by side down a muddy creek.

Men think they can handle anything. We can deal with any challenge. If it is broken, we fix it. If we can't fix it we ignore it or figure out how to live without it. I couldn't figure out what was wrong and since that is the first thing, I couldn't fix it. I wasn't even sure anything was wrong. I knew something was missing but since I couldn't find it to fix it, I resigned to trying to live without it.

My wife resigned but not so quickly. She knew there was more but probably assumed that since I didn't acknowledge anything I didn't want to change. Communication was dying at both her end and mine.

We avoided our marriage by preoccupation with jobs, the kids and hobbies. We had vacations with the kids, ate out with the kids, popped corn with the kids and took them to dance classes and swimming lessons. There was no couple, only a family.

Then one day the oldest moved out. Later the next one moved out. There was a pattern developing here. There was a frightening possibility that someday all four of them would be gone and we would be back to where we started except without that something we once had, that thing that brought us together in the first place. It was like waiting for that bullet all over again.

My work has a lot to do with people and how they get miserable. I began to realize that my wife and I were getting that way. I could figure it out in other people, so why not do it for us. I started with myself. I realized that I could be focused on clients and take an interest in their interests. Maybe something like that was called for so I looked across the living room and saw the woman I had married so many years ago. I stared at her while she sat there reading and dealing with the frequent interruptions by our two younger kids. "What do I like about her?" I asked myself, "isn't she just as interesting as my clients?"

She glanced at me and asked, "What are you staring at me for?"

"Just looking," I said. She went back to her magazine.

I continued with my experiment. I looked at her and I was struck by how really pretty she was. I looked at her eyes and hair and especially her smile. I began to get the memory of a long gone feeling. I decided that what had been missing was me. I had quit appreciating her. I knew I had to make an effort. I had to *do* something, not just sit there. I got up and went over to her chair and kissed her on the cheek.

My experiment worked. When I began to act on my best intentions two people began to have very positive emotional reactions, first, my wife and second, me. My feelings for her and for our marriage began to increase as I demonstrated them. I learned first hand that change in feelings can come through change in actions.

About Marriage

While I recognize that there are other arrangements between couples than formal marriage, I will use the word often. Those of you in other types of committed relationships will have to excuse me for that. The essential concept is commitment.

For many, marriage has a religious foundation. For others, it is a more broadly spiritual experience. Still others consider it a legal and secular condition. Regardless of how you see it, it can be a good or a bad experience depending on what the two of you put into it.

Marriage has its goals of growing mutual love, companionship and, ultimately, happiness. When these goals are being frustrated it is time to sit down and seriously look at what your goals are and where you are on the path to them.

There are problems in relationships and the most common involve dominance and control. Power is always present in relationships but it is not a problem until it is out of balance. When one person exercises too much of it, the other reacts in a negative way. Eventually, the balance of power must be restored or the lawyers get involved.

On another level, relationships are composed of interactions that can be divided into three categories: Neutral, such as information exchanges, reinforcing, such as compliments and small and large acts designed to enhance the relationship, and punishing, those actions which hurt. We need to become conscious of what we say and do and the impact those things have on the relationship.

Passion, romance and intimacy are the marks of long-term intimate relationships but they cannot be taken for granted. They have to be built by the two of you. Marriage is not a low-maintenance proposition.

Marriage might be simple if it were not for those other complicating factors like your life outside of the home, different interests, children and in-laws, among other things. You cannot avoid these complications; it is not just the two of you – marriage is a social reality.

It is All About You

I have had the honor of working with hundreds of couples and their marriages. These couples have taught me a great deal about relationships in general, theirs in particular and mine incidentally. I know that while each person is different, most relationships are governed by principles that cut across race, age and everything else.

This is a book about you and how to avoid some problems and, I hope, fix some. The focus is on you because if you try to place it on your partner you will only build resentment. This is an attitude that is absolutely essential for changing relationships.

You have to be the one who changes things. You have to be the one who makes the first move, the second move and as many others as it takes. You have to be the one who learns the principles of relationships and applies them. You have to be the one to change your own behavior.

Moreover, you have to be the one who learns to back off if you are in the wrong.

That last point is very important. Not every relationship works. No matter how much you want a relationship to work it just may not happen. You are not entitled to another person's love and if he or she, after all your best efforts, refuses to share it with you, you have to swallow your pride and pain, back off and get on with your life.

About the Book

This book is composed of two parts, The Basics, which explain some of the basic principles for making relationships work. The second part contains stories and Lessons. The stories are shortened and fictionalized for the sake of readability and to protect the identities of the people involved. The lessons are supplemental readings that are designed to add to what you have learned through previous material.

I hope this book is helpful to you. In the event you have difficulties resolving your problems you should not hesitate to see a marital counselor. All of the work will still be up to you. Make this your motto:

IF IT IS TO BE, IT IS UP TO ME!

Part One

The Basics

I know what you're thinking and you're wrong!

Chapter One
Establishing Goals

Most of us do not think of goals when we think of relationships but they are there, unspoken but powerful, nonetheless.

Someone once said to me, "If you don't know where you're going you'll probably end up somewhere else." I have come to believe that is true.

A goal can help you feel like you are in control of circumstances rather than feeling that circumstances are running you. A sense of control is essential to being a person. Those who believe that luck and forces outside of themselves dictate their lives are not capable of change because they do not have that sense of control.

I work with many depressed and stressed people and one common theme emerges, and that is that the more depressed a person is the less in control they feel. The same is true of people who are said to be suffering from a "poor self-image." They typically feel hopeless and helpless. Part of their treatment is to restore a sense of control.

Setting a reasonable goal or two is one way to start restoring that sense of control. The goal gives a person a feeling that they are going somewhere and they, not external circumstances or people, have set the direction.

Goals should be reasonable, realistic and attainable.

To set a goal for someone else's behavior is not reasonable. You are not in charge of their behavior and should not try to be. Still, I find this is one of the most common quirks I have found in working with relationships. The fault is always someone else's. When you say "Everything would be just fine if you…" you are failing to notice that your partner is saying or thinking the same thing. In my experience there is truth on both sides.

Unrealistic goals are those that demand too much or demand too much too soon. You have all heard it and perhaps you have said it: "I am going to lose (fill in the number) pounds in (fill in the number) weeks." Usually, the number of pounds is too high and the number of weeks is too low. If you are demanding that your relationship should improve overnight, you are writing your own prescription for failure. As the cliché goes, "It didn't get this way overnight, it won't get better overnight."

It is OK to have a large (and even vague) overriding goal, but small goals that lead toward that goal are more productive. Next to setting goals, achieving them brings a sense of control back into your life. That is one of the reasons you should start with a small goal that you can achieve—and achieve fairly quickly.

You want a happy relationship, right? That is a good overriding goal that you share with your partner. But it is a vague goal and vague goals are often the foundation of more conflict because each of you tends to see it differently. That's why you shouldn't stop with that big beautiful goal.

Goals should be specific.

"I want him to treat me with respect," Marlys said when I asked her for a specific goal. I explained that this is a good goal but it is not specific enough.

"How will he act when he shows a sign of respect?" I asked.

"He won't yell at me."

"Excuse me for being silly, but your gold fish doesn't yell at you. Is that respect?"

Marlys saw what I was getting at and with a little more effort she came up with a more specific picture of what she wants. "I want him to greet me when I come home and ask me how my day went."

"But," she went on, "that seems like such a small thing. There are many others."

I agreed but I explained that from this small beginning, we should see the snowball effect: his behavior will begin to spread to other things.

Goals should be positive

It is my experience that most couples think too much in terms of what they don't want and seem to have forgotten what they want.

Heaven knows, you talked a lot about the positive dreams before you got together, didn't you?

Marlys, like most of us, was starting off negative. If you are asking your partner to become more like a goldfish then you are expressing the negative. I am not saying that the negative can't be addressed but when you start on the road to change with your partner's negatives you are about to make that journey alone.

Her husband, George, can say, "My goal is not to yell at Marlys so much," but that is his prerogative. If she demands it his response will be resentment and rebellion.

The first goals you set should be positive and should ask for more of something. Most of all it should ask something of yourself or the two of you.

Shared goal setting strengthens relationships.

I always try to get the couples I work with to spend a positive hour together each week. I tell them that and I leave it up to them to figure out the details. That little benign neglect of mine to specify exactly what they will do and when makes them have to figure out the details. To do so, they will have to talk about things they like to do.

I think one of the best things a couple can do is to work together on setting goals. The goal might be to go shopping for some new faucets for the bathroom sink or just going for a ride before Christmas to look at the lights. Your goals do not have to be anything that will set the world on fire, but if you decide to do something big, that's OK, too.

That big one

You and your partner want a happy relationship. Just what is that? Do you agree on it? Have you ever talked about what that will look like when it happens? Well, it is time to do some dreaming.

"Happy" is a vague term that does not tell us much. I like a definition given to me a long time ago: "Happiness is a feeling you get when you are doing something else." In other words, you cannot make happiness a goal in itself. You can work toward creating the situations that you think might bring about this blessed state but you cannot make it happen. (By the way, happiness is not a warm puppy and love is not just never having to say you're sorry.)

You once had a dream for yourself and your partner. You and your partner talked about it for hours. You went away from those conversations in ecstasy about those things and you just knew that there would never be a relationship like yours in a million years. It's OK if you can't recall what you talked about then. You are mature now and this is a new beginning.

When your marriage is at its peak, what will it look like? What kind of things will you two be doing together? Will you have long walks on a warm evening? Will you have snowball fights and big family dinners on the holidays? Will you go to movies together or explore interesting restaurants? Will you watch a favorite old movie together or just sit on the porch together and watch the sun set? Will you listen to each other as you tell about your workday or something you saw this morning? Will you greet each other with a big hug and a kiss and say "goodbye" the same way?

If I had my wish you would put this down right now and write down all of the things you can think of and your partner would do the same. Moreover, after you had exhausted yourself writing and your partner had also, you would come together and talk about each other's ideas without censorship and with respect for how much or how little each had done. You would talk and you would listen and you would add to your ideas and eventually emerge with a common dream.

Rating

After you had agreed on the basics of your dream relationship with each other; I would ask you this question: "Are you there now?" And you would say, "No." And I would say "Do you think you can get there?" and you would be too timid to venture a "yes."

Then I would say something like this: "Give that dream the number, 100. That picture you have made is 100 percent of your relationship goal for now." Then I would ask you to tell me what percent of that goal have you attained as of today? What number would you each ascribe to your present relationship?"

There would be a moment of hesitation, maybe several, while you think about it. When I have couples do this together neither wants to offer the first estimate. Do not worry, this is not rocket science so give it a number.

Let us say you gave it a 23 percent. That is low, but it is not hopeless. In fact, it is hopeful. Now, I would ask you this: "What can you both do to bring that number up to 25 percent or higher?"

You can see that I am asking you to join with your partner and take charge. Even if your partner does not join you at first, think about what you can do to take a realistic step toward that goal. One cannot change without the other changing.

Summing up

Setting a goal for this week or this month is a small beginning but there is the snowball effect and as you take reasonable steps toward that 100 percent, you will feel the momentum growing. Soon you will find your numbers growing. Your goal is attainable. You have already described it and that pushed the snowball really hard as it gathers steam toward that attainable dream of yours.

You might feel the need to change your goals from time to time. But having a goal is healthier than not having one.

Chapter Two
Dominance and Control

This chapter is about some of the personality factors that influence relationships—often in a negative way. You will learn the importance of looking at yourself in an objective manner and addressing these issues.

Styles

Instead of looking at the depths of personality I suggest we look at what I call styles. Styles are patterns of behavior we use to attain certain goals. These styles are common to all of us and they explain how we relate to ourselves and the people around us. They are: power, superiority and amity.

The power style is the pattern of behaviors you engage in to gain control over your environment. People with this style as dominant tend to take control of situations and people. Trusting is hard so you have a tendency to keep control when it might be better to just let go.

Power people believe strongly in rules and laws. There is a right way and a wrong way and the right way is your way.

The superiority style is the pattern of behaviors you engage in to be the best, to get ahead and to win. If this is your dominant style, you will have a tendency to win at any cost, often at the cost of other people's feelings. You are highly competitive and not only want to excel, you want your kids to excel as well.

The amity style is the pattern of behaviors designed to obtain and enhance relationships and good feelings. If this is your dominant style you will care more about how people get along, not how well they perform or what the truth or rules are in any situation.

Remember, all of these styles are in your behavior, your attitudes, feeling and thinking. Probably one of them dominates. Probably one or all of them from time to time will be a source of frustration in your marriage.

If you are more of a power person, you probably have a spouse who is more of a amity person. Opposites attract, as they say, but opposites can also irritate. You want order and it seems that your partner wants chaos. Or, on the other hand, you want to enjoy life and "Ol' Stick in the mud" wants keep to the routine.

If superiority is your major style, you need to be right and you need to have the best things. My neighbor spends a lot of time doing two things, caring for his lawn and checking out other people's landscaping efforts. If someone in the neighborhood makes an improvement, he makes a better one. If this is your style, you tend to make everything a competition, whether it is your lawn or your understanding of how the world works.

Amity people tend to over-emphasize feelings and downplay achievement and obeying the rules. If this is your style, you have probably developed a great deal of sensitivity to how others feel but you have to avoid the temptation to be too lenient in child rearing. You will probably be more concerned with feelings, fun and good times than with matters of achievement, rules, routines and material things.

All of these styles have their place. Your dominant style will tend to move to an extreme in times of conflict and your partners will do the same. You have to ask yourself, in every situation, "Is my style helping or hurting in this situation." Be willing to back off.

Human animals are animals. We are born like animals, our bodies function like animals, we eat and reproduce like animals. We share some basic instincts and reflexes with animals. While we have some essential differences, we are not as far from our cousins in the animal kingdom as we would like to think.

Marking Your Territory

We human types can be as territorial as any of those relatives of ours. We also like to establish our order of dominance. In my territory, I have to exert my control. The animal in me tells me that I have to do that. It does not explain why. That is the way it is and that is it. It is often expressed as being "King or Queen of my castle," or some behavior or words that say the same thing. It also comes out in that inane phrase, "It's my way or the hiway."

Some suppose that dominance and control are totally male things but that isn't true. It is true that men seem to be accused of abusing relationships by dominating and controlling more than women do. Maybe men have more of whatever it is that causes this behavior or maybe they just are not subtle about it so they are caught.

Dominance and control have their places. For example, a boss has to exercise control and dominance to get the job done. A general has to use these in the military and we count on the police to take charge of volatile situations. Parents have to use the methods of dominance and control as long as the children are dependent on them.

If you scratch the overuse of dominance and control, you will find fear underneath. It is fear of losing things or people around you. You might fear that if you let up on your control, things will fall apart and you might suffer some loss in the chaos. So you hang on and the more you hang on the more you feel you need to hang on.

While it may come from primordial impulse, dominance does not work too well in human relationships anymore. We have progressed to the point where we can have more equality and answer our need for mutual acceptance.

Keeping the Herd in Line

Dominance means staying on top and control is the means of doing it. Control can be exercised through emotional blackmail, rage, physical pain or threat of it. It is typical that when one level of control is challenged the level of control is escalated. For example, when growling at his kids did not work, Ed started growling louder. Then he screamed. Then he screamed with obscenities. Finally, he began banging things.

The next step would be physical abuse if he had not stopped and got control of his anger.

The response to dominance is to topple it and the response to control is to escape it. Just as dominance and control are similar to behavior seen in the animal kingdom so the inclination to challenge dominance and escape control are also quite basic. In herds of animals, an up and coming male often challenges the dominant male. Eventually, he loses the head-butting contests and is no longer on top. He loses his harem and often just slinks off alone to be eaten by some other critter.

Humans have challenges animals do not have but luckily, we are equipped to meet these challenges. You cannot use the excuse that you are an animal because the species of animal you are is noted for its ability be self-directing. You can decide on what outcomes you want and you can modify your behavior to attain those outcomes.

Human animals have goals. We want to achieve emotional satisfaction through relationships. We want love and mutual respect and many goodies that animals do not have. You cannot achieve human ends with animal means, especially with those means that are detrimental to our goals. An animal behavior or attitude on one side will tend to elicit an animal response on the other. Thus, when you assume a dominant stance, your partner feels the urge to topple you. When you become controlling, your partner wants to escape or fight back.

When you are in the dominant and controlling seat you will find that you begin to act like a parent and your partner begins to act like a rebellious child. Conversely, if you begin to see your partner is trying to be domineering and controlling you feel like rebelling. In any event, the result is always more of the same. A vicious cycle is created and it is hard for either of you to back out. The dominant one cannot quit because it is hard to tell what would happen to the other if you just let go. He or she is so irresponsible. On the other hand, the rebel cannot quit because that would feel like losing oneself in the will of the dominator. What can you do? Sometimes only professional help can get you "unstuck."

Another type of control worth mentioning is control through emotional blackmail. That is when you try to make someone give in out of pity for you, sympathy or guilt. If you use pouting or "poor me" type statements you are probably controlling through this method. If you are threatening to remove your love from someone if he or she does not give in, that is emotional blackmail. It does not matter whether you use this method or a more direct one, the results are bound to be the same; you will lose their respect and their love.

Mouse on the Mirror

As the mouse said when it stood on a mirror, "That's another way of looking at it." The fact is that mice and other critters do not seem to recognize that the image in the mirror is them. They usually react to that image as another animal if they react at all.

But, you aren't a mouse and you do have the ability to see yourself in a mirror. You can even look at yourself without a mirror. You have the ability to examine your own behavior and its how it affects other people. You can be critical of yourself.

You have to be critical of yourself because sometimes your behavior and attitudes are not obvious to you. You might not realize how you are coming across to others. Worse yet, you might be defensive about it and justify that you have to be that way. It is important that you get past your defenses and take a good hard look at yourself.

If your goal is to have a fulfilling relationship with your partner, you should need no further motivation for taking this hard look. You do not have to advertise it. You can do it alone or you can do it with the help of someone you trust. Ask yourself if you issue orders a lot, if you try to control through intimidation, rage or threat. If you do, you have to either settle for being alone or you have to make changes.

I invite you to look into the mirror and see yourself, not as you would like to be but as you are, especially in the eyes of those you love.

Chapter Three
Punishing and Rewarding

When you communicate with another person, whether through words or action, you influence how someone else feels. If Joe says, "Your meat-loaf sucks!" Jane has not only received information, she has feelings because of what he said. What she does about those feelings is her choice, but there is no arguing that she did feel something.

Some new age psychologists might tell you that your feelings are a matter of choice but that ignores the fact that you do not grow up in a vacuum. You learn to have certain feelings under certain conditions. Just as you do not have a choice about feeling pain when I step on your toe, Jane doesn't have a choice about feeling pain when Joe psychologically steps on her meatloaf. She does not have to choose to feel anything because what she feels is a reflex. If she had to make a choice about her feelings, she would probably choose to feel something other than hurt.

Our social conditioning enriches our lives. It connects us at a feeling level and not just at an intellectual level. It means that we can relate to one another and not just exchange ideas. The feeling connection helps us appreciate movies, literature, poetry and music and most of all, each other. It helps us begin to understand how what we do influences how others feel.

Being sensitive to how others feel is something that exists in degrees. Some are better at it than others. Some of these become expert at manipulating other people's feelings and they become writers, artists, poets, movie creators and the like. Some become con artists or counselors.

Your capacity for sensitivity is with you when you are born. After that, you learn more. Your parents give you messages about whether it is right or wrong to have feelings and recognize them in others. They model sensitivity in the way they are sensitive to your feelings. You begin to pick it up. If your peers are sensitive to others then you will have your sensitivity deepened.

Sensitivity exists in degrees but you can develop what you have. You can become more aware of how you affect others with your words and actions.

When Joe said that Jane's meatloaf "sucks," he was delivering a hurt to her; it was like a punishment. The effect of those words was that she was hurt, sad and probably angry. What affect Joe intended we could only assume. I would assume that he meant to hurt her feelings, wouldn't you?

But sometimes it isn't so obvious. Take this example:

"When do we eat?"

That could be just a request for facts or it could be an accusation that the cook isn't doing his or her job. A lot depends on the receiver of the message. If you are in a depressed mood, you might tend to take such comments as negative whereas if you are in positive mood you might overlook some negative messages.

But the sender does have the major responsibility to craft the message to produce the effect he or she desires. You have to be aware of what you say and do and anticipate how your receiver will receive it. That sounds like a lot of effort but with a little concentration at first, it will soon become easy.

Non-verbal communication can also be very powerful. If you are talking to me and I just look away, you get the message, right? Non-verbal communication comes in grunts, sighs, sneers, yawns and a whole bunch of other gestures. And, of course, silence can very be powerful.

Mutual training cycle

Melanie, a middle school teacher I knew, told me that her mother would go into the kitchen and bang cabinet doors dishes and pots when she was upset. She would never talk about it but the message was clear, "I'm angry, stay away!" And the whole family did stay away.

Melanie's mother was training the family to leave her alone and they trained her to bang around in the kitchen when she was upset. Melanie and her family provide a good example of a mutual training cycle.

In this cycle, person A's behavior is reinforced by person B's response. B's response is reinforced by something A does or does not do in return. Let me explain further:

First, you need to understand that reinforcing means strengthening. When a certain behavior is reinforced it makes it more likely that under similar conditions that behavior will be repeated. If it again gets reinforced it is further strengthened.

The woman in front of me at the grocery checkout has a five-year-old in tow. As soon as he sees the candy displays he begins to beg.

Mother says, "No, you'll spoil your dinner."

Five-year-old continues to beg and finally begins to cry loudly.

Mother relents. (Child's behavior of crying is reinforced.)

Child quits crying. (Mother's behavior of giving in is reinforced.)

Guess what happens the next time she and the child go through the checkout? The child has taught the mother how to shut off the noise and she has taught the child to make noise to get what he wants. They are training each other. It is effective but not beneficial in the end because it teaches bad habits to both.

There is one point I have to make very clear. People do this with little or no awareness as to what is going on. This point is important because sometimes we are inclined to think that our spouse or child is behaving that way on purpose when he or she is merely doing what you taught him or her.

Spouses train each other

Every newly wed knows that the best way to hear "I love you," is to say, "I love you." Mutual training is not all bad. However, sometimes it is.

Carol complained that John did not come home right after work.

John said he hates to come home because "Carol starts in on me as soon as I come through the door."

Carol explained that she feels justified in yelling at John because he comes home late.

John avoids (puts off) the punishment his wife delivers by staying away from home. Carol feels justification by yelling at him. He trains her to yell at him and she trains him to stay away.

It turned out that even when John did come home on time, Carol would punish him. She did not see it that way. She would say something like, "Well, home on time; how come?" She did not see that as punishment but it was.

This case was changed when a new system was initiated. Carol and John agreed that he would come home every night after work except once each week when he would socialize with his friends for a couple of hours after work. They also agreed to be positive with each other whenever one came home or left. As you might expect, there were other behaviors to change but this was a good beginning.

It's hard to hug a porcupine

Rhoda and James were not getting along. She began. "I don't think we have any problems we can't solve. This counseling thing was James' idea."

James responded. "I think we have a lot of problems. She's constantly picking on me and the kids. I can't stand it any more. The kids do everything they can to avoid her. She picks on their choice of friends, their clothes, the music they listen to—just everything."

"Well, I wouldn't have to pick—as you call it—if anybody would just listen to me and take some responsibility. Besides, their music is just horrible and their clothes, their clothes—my god! Haven't you been paying any attention? My god!

"And you! You just sit there watching TV and never lift a finger to help. You dress like a slob and it's no wonder that the kids don't give a diddly damn about how they look. And you let the kids get away with murder. I have to get on them or they would never amount to anything!"

James explained that he felt "damned if I do and damned if I don't." Rhoda was very critical of just about everything her husband did and said. The same was true of the kids. When I probed further I found that Rhoda felt isolated in the family. She felt it was James and the kids on one side and she on the other.

It was a trap. The more isolated Rhoda felt the more critical she became. This led to more resistance on the part of James and the kids. Negativity keeps people at a distance. It makes you hard to like.

Rhoda learned to be more positive. She learned that criticism has its place but there are other ways to criticize. She was a perfectionist and it was hard for her to get past that. Finally she was able to show her appreciation of the efforts her family members made and to accept that it need not measure up to her expectations all of the time. She became less of a porcupine and therefore more huggable.

Catch 'em being good

You live in a negative world. You learn to look for what is wrong and ignore what is right. This is a mental habit developed over years of experiencing the same being done to you. Your teacher pointed out how many you got wrong on your spelling test and your parents generally left you alone until you did something wrong.

I propose that you turn this around. Why not make an effort to spend your attention currency on noticing behavior you would call positive and less on the negative?

Just like in the case of Rhoda, negative behavior makes others uncomfortable and it will make you less happy, too. If you tell your spouse that you like it when he or she does or says something you like, you might actually get more of it.

You do not have to get all sweet and sentimental to do this. However, it will make a big difference if you do not leave all good behavior unnoticed. Take a risk. Try it. It cannot hurt.

Banking on your relationship

I was talking to a couple who had previously seen their minister for marriage counseling. They told me he had a simple way of saying what I was telling them. He had told them that they have a "relationship bank." When they say nice things to each other, they are making deposits. When they say negative things to each other, they are making withdrawals.

I like that image. It is simple and it is correct. I would take it even farther. It does not have to be something you say, it can be something you do that deposits or withdraws. Furthermore, I have found that when a tragedy comes along it can make a tremendous withdrawal on the bank. That is why some couples have marital problems when there is a death in the family or when they have a serious financial setback.

When Fred's affair came to light it nearly bankrupted his marriage to Cathy. They were both devastated by what he had done. They had to decide if they wanted to replenish the account that he had drained or not. I have seen cases where the affair totally bankrupted the account. All of the positive things they both put into had been wiped out and there was nothing left. Why? Because they had been making smaller and smaller deposits in the months preceding the affair. At the same time, the withdrawals had been increasing.

As Cathy and Fred began working toward building their relationship I advocated that they begin to have dates and that they begin to "catch 'em being good." It worked in their case and that bank account began to grow again.

Summing up

Just like a building is made of a lot of bricks, so a relationship is made of a lot of little things. If those little things are rotten then the building will crumble but if they are strong and positive, the building will stand.

Remember: IF IT IS TO BE IT IS UP TO ME. Do not wait for your partner to begin. You begin and let your partner catch up.

I'm glad you decided to stay home with me this evening.

Chapter Four
Building Intimacy

This chapter is about that mysterious factor in every special relationship, intimacy. It is the challenge of every couple to grow in intimacy and once you have moved to meet that challenge, it becomes very addicting and you will want more.

Getting to know you

My understanding of intimacy: "intimacy is the process and result of sharing experiences of all kinds over time and space." This is the understanding that makes the most sense to me. Some people seem to think that sex is the same as intimacy but in my definition (and common experience) you can have sex with someone without intimacy. And you can have an intimate relationship without having sexual intercourse.

As you build intimacy, you gain a certain "response-ability" for that person. In other words, you develop the ability to respond to their needs and wants. You not only know in an intellectual way, you can get a feel for your partner that no words can explain. You are able to interact with your partner at a deeper level than anyone else can.

You can have instant infatuation but intimacy takes time. It takes repetition of experience together in a variety of situations. Intricate processes such as intimacy building require repeated experience and you cannot have that all at once.

I read an article once about how to create "Instant Love." The author said that you put two people in a highly stressful predicament where they have to depend on each other to get out and they will feel that they are in love when it is over. However, unless this couple gets to know each other over time, this "love" will fade and often turns into resentment.

When I say that you need space to build intimacy, I mean that you have to share in different situations. You might develop an intimacy in a working relationship where you feel you can be "in sync" with a work partner, but that lacks the breadth of the intimacy you have with a spouse where your intimacy is built in many different situations with many different people.

The core of discovery

In 1803, the United States purchased the territory of Louisiana. Thomas Jefferson called upon Meriwether Lewis and his friend, William Clark to explore it. They put together a crew that was named, "The Corps of Discovery." They set out to explore this acquisition and it took them four years to do so. They sailed, rowed, pushed and pulled their boats up the Missouri River, met many Native Americans and encountered all kinds of flora and fauna. Yet, there were miles and miles they never saw. There were whole areas of Missouri, Nebraska, the Dakotas, etc., the explorers never saw. Those places and peoples were left for others to discover. Moreover, we are still discovering new things about our West.

Oh, that's right, this isn't a history book. However, like all history, this story might have a message for us. Just as Lewis and Clark did not see the whole thing in their four years, so you have not explored the whole other person in your relationship no matter how much time you have had to do it. If you don't like Lewis and Clark, let me offer another option. How many years have people been looking at the moon? Silly question? Maybe, but my point is that we have not answered all the questions about it yet. There is more to be explored.

Who is the more intricate, the man in the moon or your partner? There are many unknowns in both cases but a living being is always more mysterious than a merely physical one. A dandelion is more complex than a rock, a duck is more complex than a dandelion and there is more to learn about your partner than there is to learn about a duck.

I recall a TV show that was based on couples guessing how their partners would respond to certain questions. The producers had the wisdom to know that there would be a lot of humor in the inaccuracy of the responses. While this game was played among newly weds, I have found in my marriage counseling that people married for twenty years are no better. The point is that there is always something more to know and experience with your partner.

The core of mutual discovery lies in openness. You each have to admit that there is something new to experience in this relationship. When you quit admitting that, you are beginning to take one another for granted and when that happens your relationship is almost dead.

Intimacy is not one sided. You cannot just let your partner do all the work as if you are worth knowing and he or she is not. Conversely, it is an omen of disaster when you are the one who is open to your partner while he or she is not open to you. Within the relationship, there is no room for prima donnas or prima dons.

Huddling in the storm

One of the first books I read on marriage contained several studies on how marriages work. One of them was about the effects of crises on marriage and family. It showed that when something bad happened, like a death, financial disaster, infidelity, loss of job, etc., the relationships suffered. In some cases, the effect of a crisis was to destroy the marriage or the family relationships beyond rebuilding.

Crisis is a Greek word that originally meant a decision point. I compare it to a fork in the road where you have to take one path or the other. Some people do not have any interest in continuing that journey together and they split when things get tough. Others seem to survive the crisis because of their relationship and they do go on together. In fact, some couples seem to get stronger because of the crisis they have survived.

What makes the difference? The difference is the degree and quality of intimacy the partners have built with each other before the crisis. In these cases the couple have been mutual in their openness to intimacy and have had their relationship tested and proven in many ways before they faced the current crisis.

In contrast, those couples that fell apart tended to have been one-sided in their relationship. When smaller crises came, one partner deserts and leaves the other to deal with it. Let me give you this example:

When their daughter was molested, Mary took her for counseling. George found all kinds of reasons for not going. In fact, he refused to deal with it at all. This was typical of George's behavior. Shortly after George's business went into bankruptcy, Mary filed for divorce. Intimacy had been one sided. Mary told me she was tired of bearing the emotional burdens alone.

Elements of intimacy

Intimacy is not all about crises. It is about sharing all kinds of experiences together. It is also about humor. Couples who have developed intimacy have a similar sense of humor. They also share little jokes that may not seem funny at all to other people.

They also have memories of all kinds of things that keep coming up in conversation. They may have had a trip to Hawaii that gives them shared memories but they also have the time when they volunteered at the soup kitchen and the time they fixed the toilet together.

Intimate partners smile in recognition when someone says something that brings back memories of an experience they shared years ago. They can look at a sunset and remember the other times when they saw such a sunset. They can hear someone else's experience and recall the time they went through something similar together.

As time goes on, they gain more experiences that bring back the feelings of other experiences and those feelings connect to still others. The growth in intimacy means that a myriad of feelings and facts has been mutually shared and others have not been part of them. The couple shares their own world, not just a physical world but a world I can only call, "spiritual."

Meeting you again for the first time

While preparing for one of my psychology classes, I found an interesting study that involved sensory studies of Zen monks. When most of us are presented with a picture we haven't seen before we have neurological excitement as measured by brain scans. After the picture is shown more times the excitement diminishes and finally reaches near zero. When these monks were shown the pictures repeatedly, the neurological measures indicated that each time they saw them they had the same high level of excitement as they had the first time.

What does this have to do with intimacy? The answer is that there is a danger in thinking that you know your partner so well that you no longer have to be open to knowing and experiencing more. The monks show us that excitement can be renewed. The biggest danger to relationships is the tendency to get bored. However, boredom is not inevitable.

Boredom is something that exists in you, not in the situation. For instance, you might feel bored if you listened to the recitation of my family history. Someone else might be fascinated. It depends on the amount of interest each one is willing to put into something.

We have a tendency to be passive in many things. We have been trained to believe that we just have to sit there and be entertained. If we are not entertained, we do not blame our inability (or unwillingness) to make something interesting, we blame people and things outside of ourselves. However, boredom is not out there. The Zen masters have proven that.

If your relationship is boring, it is because you have not put interest into it. Try today to see him or her with fresh eyes. You will be surprised.

Are you anatomically correct?

Chapter Five
Passion and Romance

This chapter is another one about the misunderstood facets of passion, love and romance. These are essential to every serious committed relationship. You have to work on these facets if you hope to make a fulfilling relationship happen for you and someone else.

A little romance

I am cynical about love after many years of listening to batterers tell me they "love her," and victims of batterers saying, "I know he loves me." Along with this is the meaningless break-up phrase, "I love him but I'm not *in love* with him." Another man justified his affair by paraphrasing the old song, "I lost that loving feeling."

I am cynical about love because it is thrown around with careless abandon. It is a useful word for seducers and con artists and under the umbrella of this word, almost every abuse in the world has been perpetrated. Love of country, love of religion, love of children, love of this or love of that—all of these and more have been the excuses for all kinds of violence and abuse humans can imagine.

Every time I hear this word used in a popular song or in a movie or TV program I cringe. I cringe because the media types seem to assume that love is not only easy it is something people are entitled to. Stalkers buy into this assumption. Because some guy "falls in love" with a woman he feels she owes him love in return. I've talked to these stalkers (both male and female) and their sense of entitlement justifies their following the target of their attention, sending unwanted gifts, making multiple phone calls at all hours. When affection is not forth coming, the stalker gets vindictive. Their target needs to be shocked into the realization that they must return his or her affection.

Before you get the idea that I do not believe in love, let me assure you that I think highly of love. The way I understand it, love is the ultimate expression of what it is to be a mature human being. It goes beyond intelligence, money, power and achievements of every kind.

I am convinced that loving is not easy. When I was a college teacher I offered a course entitled, "Love," and it filled up immediately and many students had to be turned away. These students were eager to get past the cliches about love to learn what it is really is.

What's love got to do with it?

Love is a human activity. The kind of love I am talking about is between people who accept each other as equals. Your dog might be loyal and attached to you, and as close as that might come to love in your mind, it is not. I accept that a mother loves her child and a child loves his mother but that is not our concern in a marriage book. It is not between equals.

Love grows. It starts with interest and infatuation but I do not call it love until it has time to mature. You saw your partner and became interested. You investigated and infatuation set it. Do you know what infatuation is? It is a temporary mental disturbance. If your partner feels the same, you two will probably take the relationship further. At this point, you will begin to talk about love and in no way will you accept my caution that this is a temporary condition.

Well, it is a temporary condition. God or nature created this infatuation in us so that we would end up reproducing. We might not get around to it without this initial emotional intensity and there goes the human race!

I call infatuation a mental disturbance because it is not the normal human condition. A lot of sentiments about not being able to live without the other are typical. There is a tendency to exclude other relationships and even responsibilities while you are going through this phase. You sit dreamily and ignore your work. You might ignore other people's rights and needs while you are obsessed with the object of your affections.

In time, the infatuation begins to fade but it is replaced by other sentiments. You enjoy being together but you start to lose the crazed intensity of the infatuation. You begin to fit your relationship into your life and your feelings do not interfere with work or other responsibilities. Life in general will look better than ever because of your relationship.

Then there comes the adolescence of the relationship. This is a time when you might feel resentful or even rebellious toward your relationship. You crave excitement and often look for this outside the relationship. This is not all bad. You cannot build 100% of your life around togetherness. You might find this excitement in work, in a new hobby or in sports activities. Unfortunately, you might find it in the pursuit of infatuation with another person. You might claim that you lost "that loving feeling."

I find people who are in the adolescent phase trying to escape the relationship to be with friends. While with their friends they may talk to others in the adolescent phase about the deficiencies of their partners much as adolescents complain about their parents.

When love matures, you find that you don't complain about your partner to your friends, you brag. You can be apart for a while without much discomfort and when you get back together, you are happy to see each other. You feel like you are home no matter where you are as long as you are with your partner. But most of all you share. You have your private jokes that no one else can see as funny but you can repeat over and over again.

The foundation of mature love has three elements. First, there is commitment. This is a matter of decision. You are saying, I want this relationship and I am going to hang on and even when things get boring or tough I am not giving up on it.

The second element is shared experiences over time. This is my definition of intimacy. Sexual union is one of those elements but by itself, it is not sufficient to make true intimacy. Intimacy grows with many mutually shared experiences. Traveling, paying bills, and visiting relatives, dealing with tragedies, going to concerts, doing the dishes and replacing light bulbs can all be items of intimacy. You cannot have instant intimacy.

Then there is emotion. You enjoy each other's company. You have a feeling of excitement when you see each other after a time apart. You enjoy hugs and kisses as well as sex together. You enjoy expressing your feelings to each other. Passion is an important part of your relationship.

These elements are the foundation but there is more. There is a willingness to sacrifice some of your interests and even needs for the sake of the relationship. A long-term relationship is like a rock tumbler. You take two ordinary rocks, put them in the tumbler along with some grout, and flick the switch. Over and over the rocks roll, banging into each other until the rough edges are removed. Finally, you screw off the lid and behold! Two beautify stones come out.

You take two rough and incomplete people, throw them into the tumbler of a relationship and if they hang in there they come out more fully human.

My understanding of humans is that we tend to be self-centered and less than we should be until something makes us change. One of those things is having to live in relation to others, to share and sacrifice and exert ourselves for others. Long-term relationships make us do that. In a mature relationship, we have to take into account the wants and needs as well as the rights of others. We cannot remain self-centered when we have to share our lives with others.

Beware the vampires

Of course, there are flawed relationships. There are relationships where one gives and the other takes. This does not fit my understanding of love. People can and should sacrifice for one another but when it does not help it is a waste of time. Worse than that, it is sick.

Some people are like vampires; they suck the life and goodness out of their partners. Moreover, their victims need to realize that they are not curing the vampire by letting them do it. The vampire has no motivation to change because he or she is being spoiled. The victim has to give the vampire a rude awakening.

Hate is not the opposite of love, indifference is. I have seen relationships survive all kinds of tragedies and conflicts but never have I seen one survive indifference. When couples reach the point where there is no fun and no excitement in their life; when life is just a dull routine, then their love begins to die.

Relationships are not low maintenance. You cannot just get married and let it go on its own. If you treated a car that way it would quickly fall apart on you. Relationships do, too. That is why you have to try to restore the relationship everyday.

Hot for your smile

The popular conception seems to be that passion involves hot and sweaty naked bodies. That is not wrong but it is not complete, either. Passion is emotional excitement and it need not be up to the top of the thermometer.

Passion is a special feeling you have for something or someone. In this case, we are talking about someone. If you can have passion for golf or kittens, you think about them a lot. You get excited when the topic comes up. You do not hide your passion, you are proud of it. You want to share it. You do not knock your passion and you do not like it when other people do. You exercise your passion.

When you are passionate about a person you are glad to see him or her and you are thrilled when you see him or her. You are even thrilled when thinking about seeing or hearing him or her. You are obsessed.

Of course, this is true early in the relationship, as you go through the infatuation phase. However, it can also be true of the whole course of the relationship at a different level. Yes, it is true, that fire may not burn down the woods, but it can keep a lamp burning in the window.

How can that happen? The formula is simple. Think about it and act upon it. You do not have to wait for the passion to hit you can call it up like a genie from the bottle. It is not a logical process so you cannot talk yourself into it. You just think about your partner more and you think about your partner in a pleasant way. You act upon it by doing passion. You show your partner. Do something that expresses how you feel. However, to start with, be modest in your expression. You do not want to scare anybody.

A little romance

Romance is a form of communication and communication is when you get your point across. You cannot communicate in a language your hearer does not know. When you are romantic, you are communicating your best feelings for another in a way that he or she can appreciate. The important part is how the message is received. It does not matter very much that you intended the best, the message receiver has to get your meaning.

Words are only one means of communication and sometimes they are not even the best. A smile or a touch can also be a communication. Communication can be a gesture or a gift. Sometimes a wink says more than a hundred words.

Romance is showing your partner that he or she is number one with you. Isn't that what we all desire, someone who will make us number one in their world? Moreover, mature love is the desire to make that person number one.

Romance is showing, not just thinking or feeling. Thinking and feeling are fine but if they never get out it is like wetting your pants while wearing black pants. You get a warm feeling but nobody notices. Eventually, it stinks. It is a simple fact that thoughts and feelings that are not expressed eventually die. If you do not show your love then it becomes a distant memory as the corpse of your relationship decays in front of you.

I have heard the statement, usually from persons of the male persuasion, that their partners know that they love them, they do not have to say it aloud. They claim that, "I'm just not the emotional type." I am tempted to ask them if they like sports and if they cheer for their team. I wonder if they wear jackets, banners or other paraphernalia. I also feel like asking them if they know the names of their favorite players and their statistics. Do they know their partners' shoe and ring sizes? Do they remember anniversaries? Do they know what they can say or do to make their partners feel good? Do they remember the great moments in their team's playing history? Do they know the great moments in their partners' lives?

I am certainly not against sports and I know that even these "unemotional" guys can get excited about them. However, let us keep things in perspective. That team is not going to stay up with you when you get sick or celebrate your victories.

So, why are some people so "unromantic"? The answer is that it is a case of "stage fright" in most instances. I know that sounds strange but it let me explain. Stage fright is based on a lack of confidence and fear of embarrassment. Some people avoid expressing their emotions for fear that they will be rejected or laughed at. After a while a person's ability to express emotions to a partner gets "frozen," and it needs to be thawed.

Partners of these frozen folks have to take on the burden of starting the thawing process. They need to express how important it is to have some romance in the relationship and they should not minimize it. You should plead and cry if necessary. This is not only an important issue it is crucial. Next, you should explain what you mean by romance. Illustrate it with examples from your past (make a list if you have to before hand). Try to get a commitment to try.

Finally, you should be on the alert to look for every effort your partner makes in the right direction and reinforce it. Let him know when he is on the right track. Do not wait for perfection and do not give in to the pouting complaint that, "he should know what I want," because he is trying to learn a new set of behaviors and that isn't easy.

When any of us learns a new set of behaviors we go through stages. First, we start mechanically, then it progresses gradually to the point where it becomes "natural." It is like learning to drive a car. When you learned to drive you started out that way and now you hardly have to give it a second thought. If you got no feedback for your progress you might still be walking. Be specific and clear in your expectations and explicit in your encouragement of progress.

Romance keeps your relationship alive and makes it more than just co-existence. It is essential to a healthy and happy relationship.

Great expectations

It might help to explain what romance is about with a little understanding of expectations. You enter a mature relationship with a basic expectation, to be number one to someone and to make someone else number one to you.

This expectation seems to arise from our first experience with a nurturing relationship, when we were infants. As an infant, you were dependent upon the adults in your environment for everything. As a baby you were the center of the universe and all your wants and needs were to be met upon demand—or even before demanded. You were cuddled and bathed, fed and made comfortable by the hands of parents. Your first experience of love is self-centered. As you grew, you began to recognize that you were not the center and others have their needs, too.

As you grew up you missed that time when you could be nurtured by loving people and were the center of their world. You look for ways of repeating the experience.

If you remained self-centered, you would not develop the need to love as you were loved. You would only be interested in getting, not giving. People stuck in that mode become serial lovers, going from one to another and never finding "Mr. or Ms. Right," because there is no such person. No one will be your "love zombie," as Jeffrey Daumer called it.

A related expectation is found in the desire to be respected. Respect is basic to human relationships. To be more specific, mutual respect is required in every relationship from business deals to marital harmony. But do you know what respect means?

Respect originally meant, "to look intensely." In practical terms it means to understand another's beliefs, values, attitudes, needs and wants. It means that you understand what pleases and what displeases your partner and you act accordingly. When you want to express your feelings for a person, you will know what will work and what will not.

A guy I will call, "Cal," was a workaholic. His wife wanted more of his time but he never seemed to understand that. One day his wife found a new Lexus parked in the driveway with a big red ribbon on it. She blew her top. He did not get it. He did not really respect her needs. She wanted him, not things.

When I was 10 I wanted to buy my mother some bubble gum for her birthday. My Dad clued me in that while I liked bubble gum my mother did not. It was a lesson I never forgot.

So, when you want to be romantic you find out what your partner would consider romantic. How do you figure out what that is? Take a long walk with your partner and discuss it.

Speaking of walks, one of the best things that couples can do is spend special time together. In fact, I prescribe this universally for couples who have lost the wow in their relationship. Spend an hour of positive time together once per week. Consider that an order! Do this until death do you part. Amen.

Sex—It's not just for the horny anymore

Statistics tell us that men think about sex 20% of the time. Women think about all kinds of things but about 20% of the time they say to themselves, "What's he grinning about?"

I am not going to give you detailed instructions about how to behave in the bedroom. There are other sources for that information. I will say that men and women have a great deal of difference in that area. Physiologically, men respond more quickly than women. Men are more specific-focused while women are more global. Woops! I had better explain!

A friend of mine explained it this way. Imagine a large wall. For the man there are many framed pictures on it. One frame has his family of origin. Another one has his job. Others are framed pictures of his hobbies, his friends, his children and his marriage. There is one for sex. The man can get in one frame and then leave it for another.

His wife, on the other hand, has a wall with a mural on it. There is no separate frame for sex like the one her husband has. Harvey can come home and yell at his wife and kids. Three or four hours later he wants to have sex. He messed up part of the mural and, for Ginger, the mural is ruined. She cannot understand how he can want to have sex after upsetting the household. Harvey, on the other hand, does not understand how one thing relates to another. He wants to use sex to make up.

What I mean by the woman's global and the man's specific orientation is just as I explained above. Of course, it is a generalization and, like all generalizations, it has many exceptions. I have used this example with many couples and have not found any of them who objected after it was explained.

Women need to understand that men can move into the frame of sex while all of the other parts of his life are falling apart. Men need to understand that women have a hard time doing that. Sex is not a refuge for them; it is part of the big picture.

Men can take sexual rejection very personally. Often, it is a case of celebrating his masculinity. Rejection feels like a very deep insult. It hurts. Nevertheless, men set themselves up for this, as do women, when they do not discuss it. This area is sensitive and is no area for guessing.

And, guys,

When it comes to the topic of romance, it is usually the men who have to learn something. They need to know that sex is part of the mural and that women want sex as much as they do. But women see it is part of romance. I have never met a woman who did not see being nice to the kids, her friends and her family and the even the dog and cat as romantic. It is not that all things have to be perfect. Sometimes the effort is enough.

Listen here

I will end this chapter by emphasizing that when it comes to sex and romance couples need to have long talks about it. Most of all you need to do some long, intent listening. Look at each other, take turns and LISTEN.

Remember to exercise your emotional leadership in this area.

Their special time always started with a recitation of Quincy's many faults.

HD Renshaw

Chapter Six
Relationship Strategies

This chapter offers you some suggestions for improving your relationship with your partner. You will learn to make yourself loveable if you follow these suggestions. You will also learn how to draw your partner into the relationship even if he or she is not as committed as you.

Attitude

It starts with you. This is something I have had to insist on with all the couples I worked with. I had to emphasize that point because in almost every case each partner pointed to the other as the one responsible for the problems in their relationship. "He said this, she said that" and on and on it would go if I did not stop them.

I suppose that each partner expects that I will move my chair next to his or her and join in pointing out to the other partner just what a low-down, despicable, sub-human he or she is. If I did such a thing, what would be accomplished? Nothing good, I assure you. Nothing good comes from accusations, name-calling and fits of rage. If good did come from that type of behavior there would not be any need for relationship counselors.

Have no doubt about this fact: No good comes from mutual hostility. Whenever you find yourself engaged in one of those fruitless battles, try to remind yourself that you are not building your relationship; you are tearing it down.

No positive change will occur in your relationship until you—not your partner—take responsibility for making that change. The usual response to this demand of mine is, "I have, but he (she) refuses to do so!" At that, the battle begins again. Then I tell them that they can continue to use their hostility, which has not worked, or they can try my method.

I know my clients are frustrated at me when I refuse to take sides and I refuse to deal with their complaints during the first few sessions. I do that because dealing with complaints before they have started building up the positive side of their relationship only serves to continue hard feelings. One or both will drop out of counseling if I cannot convince them to start building up their relationship strengths.

You might compare the relationship to a patient who was in a car accident. He needs surgery but he was so banged up in the accident and lost so much blood that the doctors have to stabilize him before surgery can proceed. The patient has to regain some strength so he can tolerate the stress of further operations.

I hope you will trust me enough to put your hostilities on a back burner. I know that they will not just disappear. However, whatever they are, just like the patient example, you will be better able to resolve them when your relationship is stronger.

There are two exceptions to my general rule of working on the positive. 1. If you or your partner has a drug or alcohol problem that has to be resolved before you begin working on the relationship. 2. If one of you is living in physical or emotional fear of the other that has to be resolved immediately. The number one destroyer of love is fear. I am not talking about the kind of "fear" one abusive man brought up in self-justification, "But I live in fear that she will leave me." Emotional fear is the fear of verbal and psychological abuse, not the fear that you will not get things to be the way you want them.

When your relationship is in trouble it is hard to put aside your disappointments and frustrations but that is what you should do. In doing that, you should say to yourself that no matter what your partner does or says and no matter what happens you will do your best to make the relationship better. Remember: "IF IT IS TO BE IT IS UP TO ME!"

Motivation

"If I told you to do your best to make this relationship work and I will give you a million dollars, what would you do?" I asked a couple.

They looked at each other and the woman said, "We'd work real hard at it." Her husband agreed.

"What if I would offer you ten thousand, would you still work hard?"

"Sure," she said.

"What if I offered you two thousand dollars."

"We'd work hard," the husband said.

"How about you?" I asked the wife.

"I think it would be worth working really hard for even two thousand."

"Well, I can't give you money directly, but I can promise that if you make this relationship a priority you stand a good chance of not losing that much and probably more. Have you looked into the cost of a divorce lately?"

Relationship is an abstraction to many people but money is not. There are nobler motives for making your relationship a priority, but the money factor puts it into perspective. Another way to look at motivation is this: I can guarantee you more of the same misery if you do not make your relationship a priority.

We all have priorities. We act on them. We make choices based on priorities whether we spell out those priorities or not. If your child falls and breaks a leg, your priority is obvious. You might be watching your favorite TV show or talking to friends, but this event shifts your priorities drastically. Similarly, when you decide to watch your TV show instead of listening to your partner when he or she is in distress, you are also asserting your priorities.

Priorities shift. For one month, I am asking you to consciously shift your priorities and make the improvement of your relationship with your partner your number one priority. You cannot do otherwise if you are going to make it work.

Deposits in the bank

As was already mentioned, one of the analogies used by marriage counselors is that of a bank account in which you make frequent deposits and withdrawals. The concept is simple. Certain interactions are like deposits and certain others are like withdrawals. Simple, isn't it?

Yes and no. Which interactions are deposits and which are withdrawals? Obviously, to insult your partner is a definite withdrawal and to spend a pleasant afternoon together would seem to be a deposit. Both are correct but there is more. Some deposits and withdrawals are unintentional. It does not matter what you intend, the effect is what counts.

Another consideration is that, unlike bank accounts, it is depleted over time by failing to make deposits. In fact, it is depleted very fast if it is not rejuvenated often. You cannot make a large deposit on Sunday and ignore it for a week. Large deposits are to be encouraged but small ones are just as important.

I have encountered several men (and a couple of women) who do not give compliments and do not say the magic words, "I love you." I recall one guy saying, "Of course, I love her. I pay the bills, don't I?" He is representative of hundreds of others who seem to have their romantic bones shot off in the war. They are "relationship-challenged," to say it in politically correct terminology. While they may claim that that they come from families where feelings were not expressed, they have not corrected this. They are comfortable with letting their partners carry the relationship burdens. They are also the ones who cannot understand it when their partners find emotional fulfillment elsewhere.

If this is your problem, you should get some counseling help for it. It is not healthy and it is getting in the way of your happiness.

Here are some ways you can make deposits:

Listening. The sexiest organs in your body are your ears. Take time to listen to your partner. Listen to understand. Keep your own thoughts in reserve until you have grasped your partner's.

Dating. Spend at least an hour each week together, just the two of you. Take walks, go out to eat, sit on a park bench, have an ice cream cone.

Smiling. Smile at each other. Wink.

Touching. Hug and hold hands. (Guys do not reserve your physical affection for times when you are aiming for the bedroom. Learn to enjoy physical signs of affection for their own sake.)

Surprises. Leave notes around. Buy a pack of gum, a funny card or some of your partner's favorite candy for him or her.

Compliments. Notice things aloud. Compliment the cook, acknowledge the laundry technician and praise the good looker.

Your door

I want to talk to you about your door. Your door is extremely important for your marriage and your family. When you come home do you look at the door as the gateway to love or is it portal to the infernal regions? And when you leave do you look at the door as a way to escape?

I ask you to create a new system in your family with this policy: Anyone coming through the door is greeted in a friendly way and everyone leaving leaves with a friendly "good-bye"

In between the "hello" and "good-bye," all kinds of things might happen, but there is always a little something to count on whether you are coming or going. You can count on that door meaning refuge and welcome.

So, what does this do? This is the difference between a house and a home. When all family members can count on that door, they feel comfortable with their home.

Finally

Keep in mind the mantra and say it often until in sinks in. "IF IT IS TO BE IT IS UP TO ME!"

Now, let me tell you the real truth!

Chapter Seven
Special Issues

This chapter deals with some of the leading problems in marriages. It is very general, but when it comes to problems, it is hard to get specific without knowing what your particular problems are. The answer to all problems is to build on the strengths you have, to take 100%

responsibility for making the marriage work and to not be afraid to look at your own behavior and intentions.

Money

Money is not the root of all evil. Anger over money might be. It is one of the most frequent causes of marital conflict to bring couples to the counselor's office or to the divorce court.

It is a battleground where control, amity and superiority styles clash in mortal combat. Money is a very sensitive issue. My very first counseling case involved a woman who came to my office and before she sat down she started telling me in graphic detail about the perverted sexual things her husband insisted on doing before she even sat down. When I asked her about family finances so I could set her fee based on income, she looked at me offended, "Money is private!"

What that lady said had a great deal of truth to it. Nothing is more personal than money and how you manage it.

Money is very psychological. When you think about it what is money, anyhow? Thin pieces of ornate paper can be the source of all kinds of opportunities as well as problems. However, in themselves these pieces of paper are not too useful. They make good bookmarks and you can use them to kindle a campfire if you are lost in the woods. They are symbols and symbols are psychological and cultural. Those pieces of paper mean nothing outside of their symbolic value.

Of course, those pieces of paper are powerful symbols because other people recognize them as valuable. They are what you might call secular sacraments because of that power. Besides their generally recognized value these symbols have other meanings. To some people, these pieces of paper mean power, to some people they are a means to gain advantages and to some of us, they are the means for having a good time.

Here is a simple test of what money means to you. Imagine you find a letter in the mail. You open the envelope and a check for $1000 falls out. A letter from an attorney tells you that an anonymous donor has decided you should have this. Now, without thinking about it, what is the first thing you think of? How would you use it? Your answer shows what money means to you.

If you want to use it to pay bills, you are probably a person who values security above all and money helps you attain that security.

If that money looks like an opportunity to have fun or make others feel good, you see money as a means for feeling good.

Can you see the problem if the two happen to be married? (And I should add that it is typical that security oriented and feeling oriented persons are attracted to each other so this scenario is more likely than not.) A fight is likely.

A couple I worked with was on the verge of divorce. He and she fit the model I have just presented and each was certain that there was no way their problems could be resolved. As in most similar cases, the conflict over money spread to every other area of their relationship. They complained about conflicts over children, in-laws, sex and even politics.

The solution was too simple. I suggested that they make a simple budget. Each would get an allowance to use for their own personal wants and needs and the rest would go into household expenses, savings, etc. I started with the allowances and they surprised each other with how easy it was to agree on that issue. Their requests were reasonable. After that, we had a few sessions to pick up other pieces and the last I heard was a thank you note I got a year later saying they were enjoying their marriage.

Sometimes couples need to get special help on their budgeting. This is true when both lack the discipline to live on a budget. I urge you to get special help if this is your situation.

In-laws

As a parent, I can tell you that it is hard to let go of children and it is hard to quit feeling protective of them no matter how old they are and how they feel about it. The same was true with my own parents. Even when I had a family, administered an agency and had years of experience in counseling, my mother still tried to give me the benefit of her wisdom.

Some parents are able to grow up with their children and appreciate them as equal and different individuals. When kids grow up they have their own thoughts and values and they have something to give as well as take.

Some grown up kids have found they actually enjoy their parents and vise versa. They enjoy spending time together. As with any other thing, excess can be a problem. My rule is that if anything takes away from the relationship it can be a problem. I'm not saying that a couple should spend all of their time together but if one partner feels cheated by how the other is using his or her time, it needs to be discussed.

You can divorce your spouse but you cannot divorce your family. And neither can your partner. There are certain things you just do not mess with and family is one of them. As long as the relationship with family is not taking excessive time away from your relationship it is best to accept the relationship.

However, what if the in-law relationships are negative to the relationship? In more cases than there ought to be, in-laws meddle in a couple's relationship. They never let their child grow up and feel that they have to keep stepping in to protect their poor little darling.

Speaking as a parent, as my girls grew up I kept fearing that my daughters would never meet a guy like their father. Then, as I looked back on my younger days, I began to fear that they would! Finally, when I grew up, I learned to appreciate my children's judgment and it worked out fine. Parents of adult children have to learn to let go.

Some parents do not grow up as their children do. Then it is up to the children to set limits for them. "Mom, our marriage is between us. You have to stay out of it. I love you dearly, but there are limits." You can say the same thing to Dad and to Brother and to Sister as well as cousins, aunts, grandparents and uncles.

When you get married you establish a new system and it takes priority over the one you have left. You can and should (in most cases) maintain a loving relationship with members of your former family but you are building a new one and if relationship with your family of origin is detracting from it you have to make hard choices.

Children

Insanity is inherited; you get it from your children.

The biggest anger-producing problem with children is discipline. Couples often disagree heatedly about what rules to set and how to enforce them. The stricter one parent gets the more lenient the other one becomes.

Let me tell you something that might surprise you. There is no single absolutely correct way to raise children. I used to think that there was a correct way but I was wrong. So, if you take a parenting course, it is probably OK and the same is true for books you might read on the subject.

Some parents raise children like a general runs the army. Children have to instantly comply and respond with "Yes, sir" and "No, sir." They rise at 0630 and beds are made by 0700. Morning mess is promptly at 0730 and so on until taps at 2200. Chores are assigned and are completed on time, etc., etc.

Other parents are at the other end of the spectrum. The children are given few chores. Getting out of bed, cleaning up and eating breakfast occur roughly at the same time each morning. Bedtime is about the same time each night but can vary. Beds may or may not be made.

Each approach can produce healthy adults and that is what the goal of parenting is, isn't it? As long as the parents (and I include stepparents) stay within the general guidelines major harm will not be done.

Here are those general guidelines:

Be consistent. This means that what you keep promises and that if you promise a consequence that promise is kept, too.

Be consistent between yourselves. Children need to know that what Momma says, Daddy says. Let them know that if one parent makes a decision it is only final when the other one agrees. That way they will have a hard time playing one against the other.

Be flexible. Rules and schedules are made for children; children are not made for them.

Spend special time. Children want to have your time more than your money.

Actions speak louder than words. Show them your values in action and lecture very, very little.

Catch them being good, not just being bad. Use praise and attention.

Social life

The symbol used for marriage is overlapping rings. I think that is a very good symbol because it tells us something. Each ring overlaps with the other. That is the special area of the relationship. However, there is another part of the symbol, the part where they do not overlap. That tells me that each life has another part that does not overlap.

You have interests that you do not share with your partner and your partner has interests not shared with you. John might bowl while Margie does not. Margie might like archery, but John might have no interest at all. John and Margie might have friends that are not shared, as well. As long as these interests do not narrow that area where the rings overlap, that's fine.

The problem arises when these interests take away from the relationship. When you get into a committed relationship all other relationships have to get a lower priority. Too often a person marries and continues to live life just like he or she did when single. That will not work. Marriage is not low maintenance. You cannot just get into that relationship and hope that somehow it will act like a perpetual motion machine.

A special area is socializing with members of the opposite sex. Humans have a strong "urge to merge" and it does not disappear when you get married. Jealousy can raise its ugly head, and even if there is no cause for it, it can do a lot of damage. I am not saying you cannot have a friend of the opposite sex but you have to be very careful that it does not take something away from your main relationship.

Alcohol and drugs

Alcohol consumption evolves. Many people try it when they are young. Some go on to drinking a great deal and then sort of grow out of it. Others do not grow out of it. Some of those are lucky enough to get sober when he or she is older.

It is no secret that alcohol impairs judgment and reflexes. Anything that impairs your judgment can impair your relationship. Many a couple has come home from a party not speaking to each other over something one or the other said or did there under the influence. The police will tell you that alcohol consumption is often part of criminal behavior and I know that many batterers have shown up in counseling with the excuse, "It was the alcohol…"

Many people can consume alcohol with no problem but if it becomes a problem, the only thing to do is to get an assessment for alcoholism and take treatment. A friend told me that he turned his life around when a counselor asked him, "Can you have fun without drinking?" He told me that he could not think of single instance when he had a good time without alcohol. He went on to attend AA and has not had a drink in over three years. You might ask yourself that same question.

Drugs? Why would you want to jeopardize your relationship by doing something illegal? People on drugs don't build intimacy, they just think they do. Drugs are expensive, mind altering, deceptive and against the law. Do not risk it.

Religion

I have seen all kinds of religious differences make no difference in intimate relationships. On the other hand, I have seen religion used as a battleground when the real issues are being avoided. A person will make religion an issue when they want to be self-righteous, to have God on their side. Thus, to not go along with me is to go against God and that makes you absolutely evil.

My view of religion is one in which there is tolerance and forgiveness. Religion can be a great help in relationships when it is not used as a battleground, justification or way of getting power.

If you are fighting over religion, you should get some counseling because nine times out of ten it is not the religion, it is something else.

Part Two

*Stories and Lessons for Your
Relationship*

Aimee and Doug
Superiority

Doug was referred to me by a marriage counselor for anger management. It was refreshing to see that he admitted that his anger was a major problem in the relationship and he had to take responsibility for managing it.

Doug Knight had received an athletic scholarship to the state university. He had wisely used this scholarship to forward his education, graduating with a degree in business administration. He went to work for a large insurance agency and after only two years he worked his way into a management position. After another two years he quit the agency and started his own management consulting firm which he ran from his home office. His work required him to be out of town several days each week.

Doug met his future wife, Aimee, in college. They married right after he graduated and his wife dropped out with two years to go to complete her studies in elementary education. A year later they gave birth to twin girls. They decided that Aimee should stay home with the twins until they were in school. After that, Aimee was to change her major to business and complete her degree.

"At least that was my understanding," Doug said, "but she has a different story now. Now that the kids are in school, she and her friend want to start a business of their own designing and making dresses. She wants to do it in our basement. That wasn't the plan we agreed on, you understand."

"So, the anger comes from this disagreement?" I asked.

"Yes, mostly. When I make an agreement I stick to it, you understand. A deal is a deal. We agreed on working together, building a family and a business together. I was very upset when she backed out of the deal."

"You were angry because you had dreamed of working with your wife as a partner and now that won't be. Is that right?"

"You got it. My dreams were shattered. Everything I planned went right down the toilet, you understand."

"Can't you accept that your wife had a change of mind after all this time? After seven years of marriage, raising kids and a thousand other things have happened that made things look different to her."

"I guess so, but this was a basic agreement, you understand. It was like it was part of our marriage contract, see?"

"Doug, you might see it as part of the marital agreement, but obviously, Aimee doesn't see it that way. In terms of contract law as I understand it, you don't have a real meeting of the minds. Do you see that?"

"I thought we did at the time we agreed on it. She said she would go along with it then, you understand. She seemed to like the idea then. I just want her to try my plan to see if she would like it. She won't even consider it."

"Did you hear yourself? You said it was *your plan*, right? I think it was *your plan* and I think it might have sounded good to her at that time when she was starry eyed about your future together. If you want your marriage to work don't you think you need to accept the fact that your original understanding of doing business together isn't going to happen?"

"I have a hard time letting go of this. I've been planning for this since college. When I make plans I work hard to complete them, that's how I work and that's how I think. That's even how I play. If I set a goal for myself, I do everything possible to achieve it. I thought she thought that way, too, you understand. This is almost like infidelity to me."

"Infidelity! That's a pretty strong word."

"I know. But I can't get my point across without a strong word, you understand. I've used that word with Aimee. I said, 'Aimee, can't you just understand that this is like infidelity to me.'"

"What does she say?" I asked.

"She usually says nothing. She just sits there like a dummy while I try to drill it into her head. It doesn't work, no matter how often I do it, you understand."

"And I have a feeling that in the process of trying to 'drill it into her head' that you get very angry as if being louder and meaner you can get it across where your reasoning cannot. Is that correct?"

"Yeah, I guess so."

"You keep drilling but it doesn't work, is that right?"

"Yeah, I guess so."

"Have you considered that perhaps it just isn't going to work and that you need to quit?"

"And try something different to make her understand?" he said.

"No. I think you need to ask yourself a very important question. Is it more important for you win or to have a loving relationship with your wife? Which will it be? You can't seem to win so do you want to drop that issue and try to win as a husband and father?"

It was very hard for Doug to let go of his fixation on his family business plan. He struggled with this for several sessions but he was successful. His marriage counselor told me that Aimee appreciated the effort he was putting forth.

There were other points we had to work on such as his having unrealistic standards for household chores and his tendency to accept nothing less than perfection out of his children. He also had an implicit attitude of superiority toward his wife that was very hard for him to come to grips with. His denial mechanisms were very well developed.

I am pleased to report that Doug did have success in dealing with these things, too.

Comments

Doug's greatest strength and weakness was his strong achievement style. Once he could set his focus on improving his way of relating to his wife and children he quickly made improvements.

If you find yourself trying to "drill things into people's heads" or "make them see things as they are" or "be logical" then you have an attitude of superiority. I know, you call it anything but that. But listen to the words you use. Are they words that imply that they are stupid or ignorant? Do those words imply that you have superior knowledge, wisdom or insight? Do they imply that there is only one correct way and it is the one you have chosen?

Do people avoid stating their points of view because you always have a better one? Do you always have to have the best or the most? Do you have to have the last word? Do you find yourself lecturing to people and calling it conversation?

The hardest thing for a human to do is to take a long, hard and critical look at himself or herself, but that is something you have to do in order to identify the challenges standing between you and becoming who you can and should be.

The hardest things for achievement types is admitting that there are other legitimate points of view and other definitions of success. Once that obstacle is hurdled, they can bring out their amity side.

Bert and Helen
Dominance

Counselors try to be in the middle in relationships. I tell my clients that I am trying to help them fix my real client, the relationship, but there are times when I have to put this neutrality aside in the interest of the marriage or for the safety or wellbeing of one or the other.

Bert and Helen had an on and off relationship. They would get together, sometimes moving in together but then they would start arguing and would split up. She finally began buying her own house and he took that as an assault on their relationship. Let us look at their arguments:

Bert said, "You think you will just use me and then have your little house to go hide in instead of settling things."

"Settling things? We never settle things we just go on fighting. I'm getting sick and tired of your tirades and I see no reason to stay there and let you go on cussing and calling me names."

"We can never settle anything if you don't listen to reason. Why can't you just think for a change and not go on thinking like a dumb broad all the time!" Bert continued.

Helen grabbed a tissue from my desk and turned away from Bert.

"Wait a minute," I intervened, "You can't get anywhere putting her down like that."

"Like what?" Bert said.

"You said she doesn't listen to reason and she is a 'dumb broad'. Don't you think that amounts to disrespect?"

"No, I don't," Bert replied, "not when that is exactly what she is. Besides, I said she was *like* a dumb broad when she acts like that. I expect her to be better than that. If she doesn't want to be called a dummy she should quit acting like one!"

Helen remained silent and took another tissue.

"Bert, listen to yourself. Look at Helen. Your words have had a negative affect on her and your relationship," I said.

"And what about me?" Bert replied, "Don't you think I am hurt when she refuses to listen to reason?" With that, he turned to Helen and said, "Why can't you see things like I see them; like the rest of the world sees them; like God sees them?"

(I have to pause here and tell you that last phrase is an exact quote, believe it or not.)

Realizing that this line of discussion was getting no where, I decided to try something different. Helen was obviously too distraught to join in so I proceeded with Bert.

"Bert, what would you say are the main issues you two disagree on?"

"Her kid for one. She has this son whose Dad doesn't take any interest in him and so she feels sorry for him and buys him everything he wants and won't discipline him at all. I say he should do some things around the house and she takes his side."

"How old is her son?"

"How old is he, Helen, 12 or 13 or 14?" Bert asked.

"Joey's eleven," Helen sniffed with out turning around.

"Well, he's old enough to do some things, don't you think?" Bert asked turning to me.

"What kind of things?"

"Like dishes, or mowing my lawn and stuff like that. He should be able to keep his room picked up and not go whining to Momma when I ask him to do something."

At this, Helen turned around in anger and said, "Yeah, like calling him names and kicking at him is supposed to make him feel like cooperating. Joey hates you and I think he has good reason!"

"Damn it!" Bert growled, "He ought to be damned grateful to have a place. I let him watch the TV and stuff, don't I? You'd think he'd take some responsibility when he's under my roof and if you'd quit babying him he wouldn't be such a pain in the ass!"

"That's why I got a house of my own, so Joey and I can have some peace and quiet instead of listening to you yelling and cussing all the time," Helen said.

"Well, you can take your house and your damned kid and live happily ever after, as far as I'm concerned. I'd like some peace and quiet, too, and that damned kid of yours keeps us both stirred up."

Helen turned to me. "This is just like all our fights. Bert hates Joey and Joey hates Bert. I am stuck in between. Bert has resented Joey since he came to live with us, three years ago. His Dad got married and did not want him around. Joey came to our house wounded and Bert just said, 'Get over it, kid; life is tough.' From then on it went down hill."

"Life is tough and you aren't doing him any favors by babying him and treating him like a flower. He'll probably end up queer!"

"Bert, have you always had a problem with Joey?" I asked.

"We got along fine before his Dad kicked him out and now that little kid does everything to stir up fights between us."

"You know, it is a bad thing to try to get between a mother and her child. It's a formula for losing," I responded.

"Given the fact that Joey is a permanent part of his mother's life and will be with her for the next six or seven years, are you willing to work out a way of relating to him that doesn't involve hostility? I'm asking if you value the relationship more than your resentment of Joey?"

This caused Bert to think a moment and when he answered it was a repeat of the hostility he had already shown. I tried posing the question other ways but I always got the same response. Bert was not going to give an inch. He could not conceive of dealing with Joey any other way.

"Then your position is that it is either you or Joey; Helen has to choose. Is that right?"

"I never thought of putting it in those words but I guess that is what I'm saying. Helen has to choose."

"I never thought you would say such a thing," Helen said.

This time, Bert was silent. Finally, he just put his hands up and said, "I guess it's over." With that he walked out of the office.

I looked at Helen. I expected she would be crying again but she didn't show any emotions. After a few seconds she spoke. "You know something; I feel relieved."

"Relieved? Why?" I asked.

"Bert has always had it his way and I went along with everything he wanted. I didn't realize how unhappy I was with him. You know, I don't think Joey wanted to break us up but it took this crisis to make me realize how miserable I was with Bert. When you simplified it I felt like you were saying what I really believed deep down but would never admit."

Comments

It was obvious within the first few minutes of our session that Helen was miserable and she was trying to convince herself that this relationship could work. The human mind has the ability to try to reconcile contradictions as in Helen's case. This quirk of human nature can explain a lot of strange human behavior.

As it turned out, Helen had left her previous marriage with what you might call a "poor self-image." She lacked a sense of worth and felt vulnerable. Bert came along and was able to use that to dominate her. At first she was convinced that he was the one for her, strong and firm in his beliefs and standards. She looked up to him as a protector and guide. As she submitted to him she felt lucky to be wanted by such a man. The misery came gradually. She doubted the value of her feelings, values and needs. She lived in Bert's shadow for years.

When Joey came to visit she hoped that they would be a family but Bert couldn't tolerate the competition for her attention. He would probably not admit that. When I asked him the crucial question, I brought out the words neither he nor Helen had actually said but deeply felt. Once those words were brought out into the open, this couple was free to separate permanently.

Helen needed a few more sessions just to affirm her as she began to reclaim her lost sense of worth.

Bert could have learned a lot about relationships but as far as I know, he did not pursue it.

Carla and Marco
The anatomy of miscommunication.

The nursery was originally Carla's idea. Marco worked in his family's dry cleaning business. Carla had worked at various jobs but wanted something of her own. She started off growing African violets in their basement and from there she expanded to other flowers and plants. Within two years she was working full-time at her own nursery business. In the third year, Marco, who had helped out in his spare time, began working full-time at the nursery and occasionally helping out at the dry cleaning business.

Marco had primary custody of two children from a previous marriage. Nicole was 12 and Andrew was 10. Both were good students and generally presented no problems for their father and stepmother.

The problem Carla and Marco brought to counseling was a conflict over the children. Carla explained:

"We both work all day, long hours and by the time we get home we are both exhausted. I don't think it would be too much to ask the children to do some chores around the house. But he wants to baby them and make excuses for them. They are his perfect little angels who can do no wrong."

"That's not true!" Marco said, "They're just kids. She thinks they ought to act like little Nazis doing exactly as she orders and never having any fun! And she gives orders the time."

"He's lying!" Carla said, her voice rising, "He knows I love those kids. I don't expect them to be perfect, just help out a little. And they would, too, if soft old Daddy, their hero, didn't swoop down to rescue them from the mean old bitch of a wicked stepmother!"

At this point I intervened and tried to get the yelling down to a reasonable level. I asked them more about their backgrounds and tried to get them to specify their goals for the counseling. I have to admit that I did not have much luck. The arguing and accusations would flare up like the embers of a forest fire and I had to try to stomp them out before they got too destructive."

I did lecture them about one of the pet peeves of every counselor: "When you two argue you aren't arguing in a productive manner. One of biggest mistakes you both make is to pretend to read each other's mind. You both say that you know what the other one thinks and you characterize that in the worst way. This only serves to intensify the response you get. I urge you to examine yourself and not let that happen again. Maybe you will not be able to actually communicate until you quit turning these discussions into battles."

I did not think that lecture would do much good and I was right. The next session was a repeat of the first one with more details. I gave the same lecture again.

Before the third session, Carla called me. She had moved out of the house and was living with a friend. She said she did not want to return until Marco apologized to her for the things he said. I urged her to keep the next appointment. I called Marco at work and told him that it was important for him to come to the appointment also. He said he would but he was becoming very discouraged.

Counselors prepare for their appointments and try to devise strategies for their sessions. I have to admit that I was coming up empty on this one. I decided to punt. By that I mean that I was going to get into the session and not put out fires anymore. I was just going to let them go and wait for inspiration.

Carla and Marco came in and sat down in silence, looking away from each other. I began by telling them that I wanted them to argue. "What set you both off when Carla decided to move out?"

"She said that Andrew didn't pick up in the living room like she had demanded that morning when we went to work. She got on his case and called him names."

"I asked him to clean up the living room and he shrugged. Then I told him I expect it to be done today. He just walked away. I left it at that."

"She did not," Marco added, "She got on him like ugly on an ape. She couldn't shut up about it. We got home from work and the battle started. I couldn't just let her pick on him that way so I asked her to calm down."

"Hero Daddy to the rescue again. He always undermines my authority right in front of those kids and I'm tired of being made into the evil bitch stepmother time after time."

"Well, if you would just deal with them in a civil manner, I wouldn't have to rescue anybody. You act like a damned bitch so don't get upset when you feel like one."

"See, he called me a bitch! You call that love? Why the hell should I stay in a situation where I'm treated that way? He doesn't want his little darlings to lift a finger and I try to give them a sense of responsibility so they'll grow up right and I get slapped in the face. Call me a bitch? I'll be a bitch, then."

"I didn't call you a bitch," Marco said.

"You sure did, didn't he? You heard him."

I raised my palms signaling neutrality.

The argument went on and more names flew. They got louder and louder and meaner and meaner. I listened until I had heard enough and then I yelled at the top of my voice, "SHUT UP!"

I should tell you that I am a very quiet guy. Those who know me know that I do not get upset and never (hardly ever) get loud. So when I yell I get attention. My secretary, down the hall told me later that she spilled her coffee because of my roar.

They did shut up and stared at me. I let the silence take effect for a couple of seconds before I began. "You two have one major problem. You do not listen. I've been listening to you two for the past half hour and I think both sides have valid points. If you two would just listen you would find that you are making a lot of assumptions about what the other person's position is and you are wrong."

"Now, I want you to take turns listening—not arguing—<u>listening.</u> Ok, you first, Marco. What do you want Carla to understand?"

"I want her to know that I don't like the way she talks to Andy and Nikki sometimes."

"OK, let's stop with that for now. That is what I heard you saying. Now, Carla, what do you want Marco to understand?"

"I love the kids. I just want them to take some responsibility around the house."

"That's good, Carla, let's stop with that for now. Marco, did you understand what Carla said?"

"Yes, she wants the kids to do all the housework."

"That's not exactly what she said. She wants them to take on some responsibilities in the home. Is that right, Carla?"

"Yes. I don't think they ought to do everything, just a few chores. I don't think that is unreasonable."

"Now, Carla," I said, "Do you understand what Marco wants?"

"He wants me to baby the kids."

"I'm afraid you didn't listen any better than Marco did. I think Marco has no problem with the idea of chores, he is concerned with the way you talk to them. He implies there is a better way. Is that right, Marco?"

"Yes. I think that the kids should do chores but I think that Carla could talk to them nicer."

"Carla, do you think that Marco might have a point about the way you talk to the kids?"

"Well, I guess so."

"OK, you two agree that the kids should have chores and you agree that they should be talked to better. Is that right?"

They both nodded.

"Do you agree that you haven't been listening to each other?"

They nodded again.

"Well, I am going to suggest two remedies to your marriage problems if you agree. Number one, I want you to attend parenting classes at the Y together. Number two, I want you to continue in counseling and first we'll work on building your communication skills. Do you agree?

They did agree and, after some more counseling, I am happy to report that this marriage, at last report, was still going strong.

Comments

Communication is one of the biggest problems in marriage. Counselors hear about money problems, sex problems, in-law problems and a whole bunch of other problems. But the most common problem is communication.

The biggest problem in communication is listening. Like Carla and Marco, couples are too angry and defensive to take time to listen. It becomes a verbal contest in which each wants to score the most painful point on the opponent. If you just take the time to listen to the other point of view until you understand it, you might learn that there is little or no disagreement.

It is hard to be angry with someone who listens. In fact, listening is one of the great diffusers of anger. I recommend that you practice listening at every opportunity.

Cathy and Fred
Surviving an affair.

Fred called for the appointment and asked to see a counselor alone, before his wife came in. I agreed but told him I wanted to see her with him very soon.

Fred was an up and coming young executive in a large insurance company. However, when I first saw him he came from home and was dressed in jeans and a sweatshirt. He was unshaven and obviously had not spent any time on combing his hair. He did not smell bad, I was glad to discover.

"Well, Mr. Renshaw, I really messed things up," he began. I don't know if I have a marriage anymore. I don't know how I could be so stupid."

"Go on, Fred, I'm listening."

Fred went on to tell me that he had an affair with a secretary in his office. It had started out with working together on a project. They had to work late and when it came time to go to the head office with the project, the secretary had to accompany him. All of this closeness led to sharing how dull their marriages had become and, "Before we knew what was happening we were in the backseat of my car doing everything you can imagine like a couple of kids on a prom date.

"After that, we were both ashamed. She's married, too, and she has two children. I have one. We cried and promised it would never happen again."

"But?" I wondered.

"It did happen. We began to gradually find ways to meet again. I would tell her I had to go to the Mall and she would show up. Then it was back to my car. One time we splurged and got a motel room. Then I had a business trip and she told her family that she was going to visit an old friend and we got two days in a motel."

"So, how did this come to light?" I asked.

"About a month after we went on that business trip the credit card bill came and my wife did some checking and found out that I had rented a room for two. She called my friend's husband and they both confronted us."

After that, Cathy left Fred. "I got home from work and she had left me a note that she was taking Molly and going away somewhere. She said she had a lot of thinking to do and she might be back."

Fred had one question, the usual one: "Why did I do it?"

Why people have affairs is a question that leads to other questions. In all my years of counseling couples I have never found the answer to that question. There is no single answer. In trying to help clients come to terms with this issue I tell them that we are attempting to solve a jig saw puzzle. It is like the one your grandmother may have given you when you were visiting her as a child. You might find some of the pieces or maybe most of the pieces but probably not all of the pieces.

Some of the puzzle pieces include stress, opportunity, self-image, self-control, early experiences, the quality of relationship with your spouse, characteristics of the "lover," attitude toward the opposite sex, etc.

There are some people who are habitual offenders. They seem to be unable to commit to a monogamous relationship. They have been called "sex addicts" but no matter what the label, these people are very destructive to anyone they become involved with. They are good a seducing their targets and they enjoy the power they have over others with their sexuality.

However, most of the people who end up having affairs are not sex addicts. They are generally normal folks who let themselves fall into these predicaments and want out. You could give them every psycho-logical test and assessment under the sun and you would never find any pathology that would label these folks as abnormal in any way.

One of the biggest puzzle pieces is this one: an affair rekindles that old feeling of infatuation you had with your first love. That feeling is always there in the beginning of a romantic relationship. It is intoxicating, it is absolutely wonderful. And it is addicting. And it doesn't last.

Fred told me that the romance went out of his marriage and he and Cathy became more like roommates. She worked, he worked and they picked up their daughter from the sitter came home fixed a quick meal, plopped in front of the TV for a while, put their daughter to bed and eventually went to bed themselves. Day after day they did the same thing. Sex was routine and done out of obligation. Occasionally they went out with friends, but mostly they stayed home. He played golf on Saturdays and she bowled on a Tuesday nights.

When Fred was given the task of working on the company prospectus his boss assigned his own secretary, Lisa, to assist him. Much of their work had to be done after regular business hours so that they were often alone in the office. They started talking about personal matters and they soon began to feel those old feelings of infatuation. It was all down hill from there.

Fred and Lisa both had let their marriage become dull. Their new found thrills kept drawing them back together not so much because they loved each other but because they loved the thrills. If you asked them at the time if that was what was happening they would deny it. They would talk about the things they had in common and about how wonderful the other one was.

But don't ask them because they are nuts. Infatuation makes them that way and no one is less capable of self-understanding than someone who is nuts. They have experienced emotional highs and the natural result is to justify their "love."

The people having the affair are living in a fairy tale. They do not have to argue over who takes out the trash and they do not have to deal budgets. They are living an adventure. They share a wild secret and they conspire together to keep from getting caught at it. All of the cloak and dagger stuff just adds to the enchantment and keeps the thrill alive.

But there is also guilt. They feel guilty because they know they are betraying their partners and their own values. To ease the guilt they go through all kinds of mental gymnastics. They look for faults in their spouse especially neglect or disrespect. As Fred put it, "If she's ignoring me then it's her fault that I seek comfort elsewhere." He still knew that he was lying to himself.

The innocent partner

Guilt is not the sole property of the guilty party. The innocent party often feels that he or she has failed in the relationship. After all, as Cathy put it, "Why would he look elsewhere if I was a good wife?" The fact that Fred had an affair stimulated her old insecurities and she doubted her worth as a woman.

Of course, she was angry, too. He had made vows and they even had a daughter. Didn't he even care about her? "Why did you risk Molly's happiness for that woman?" She asked him.

Fred had no answer for her. As I said, Fred was nuts. People who are nuts don't think right.

"You were just thinking of yourself, weren't you?" she said.

Of course, he was. People who are nuts are not known for their concern for others.

By the third session, Cathy had joined us. She was angry, confused and hurt, to say the least. She had not yet returned to their house. She announced that she was not sure she would ever come back. Still, I could see that she wanted her marriage fixed.

Cathy had a string of "Whys" to ask Fred. She would ask, "Why did you have to have an affair? Why didn't you think of me and your vows?

Why didn't you think of Molly? Why didn't you tell me what was wrong with me?"

Fred had a hard time enduring these questions. Cathy would ask them at every opportunity and Fred would try to give her an answer but he admitted he did not know what caused him to have an affair. She would ask about details of the affair and then she would ask what was wrong with her that he should seek another woman. She asked these kinds of questions repeatedly.

In our individual sessions, Cathy would ask me similar questions. Cathy had to ask those questions in order to ease her anxiety. She could not deal constructively with the situation until she had done so. I was patient with her until she started running out of "why questions." Then we could move on.

The biggest question is not "why?" but "How?" How do you insure that it won't happen (again)? Cathy finally started asking the "how" questions.

"How can I be sure the affair is over? How can I be sure he loves me more than her? How can I ever trust him again?"

Trust is a hard issue. It requires one element that counseling can't provide—time. Once trust is broken it takes time to heal that break. The person who is responsible for that break has to take on the task of being accountable for his or her time and actions.

The other thing that is essential is that the couple start their relationship over. The greatest assurance of continued fidelity is to strengthen that relationship. It is not a case of restoring the relationship; a new one needs to grow where the old one died.

I haven't said anything about forgiveness. I do believe it is necessary but, as Cathy said, "I just can't forgive him—at least not right away." That is correct. Forgiveness isn't easy. It isn't a case of "forgive and forget," because you won't forget. And probably you shouldn't.

The offender needs to continue to remember how close he or she came to losing the marriage, not to kick him or herself around about it but to keep alert and to keep gratitude alive.

What happened to Cathy and Fred? Well, they went through a couple of months of counseling with me and then we decided that they were ready to continue on their own. The following Christmas I got a card from them and it had a family picture on it. Their only message was, "Thanks."

Dean and Emily
Control through weakness

Control is a dirty word in the discussion of relationships. It is associated with the mean spirited tyrant, usually a male, who dominates his partner enforcing this control with real or implied physical violence. But control exists in all relationships and it is usually much more subtle than the violent type. We all influence each other and that is a type of control. I may tell you I have a headache. This may limit the amount of noise you make. This is control with your consent and consent of some level is always present in cases of control.

The case of Dean and Emily illustrates how weakness can be used as a means of control.

Dean and Emily had been married six years. They had one child, a daughter named Ginger, who was five. Dean was a teacher in an elementary school and Emily worked as a church secretary. When they came to the first counseling sessions I was impressed with their intelligence and sensitivity. I began as usual, asking for a statement of what they wanted from couple counseling.

"We want to learn to meet each other's needs better. You see, we agree on one thing and that is that we are not making each other happy." Emily began.

"To be more specific, we disagree over the amount of time I spend with my friends. She wants me to be home all of the time and I think we both need our own separate time," Dean added.

"But, didn't we marry with the idea of being together? Isn't that what we wanted. Marriage comes before friendship, doesn't it?" She addressed the last question to me.

"I do not wish to join either of you," I said, "counseling involves a certain amount of neutrality. I need to know more about your relationship. Besides this problem, are there any others?"

"Sometimes he doesn't seem sympathetic to me. Sometimes I'm so upset that I cry and he just walks out of the room. I feel so alone and neglected. Maybe he wants another woman." Emily picked a tissue out of her purse and held it to her eyes.

Dean reached over and put his hand on her shoulder. "I don't want another woman, Emily, you know that."

She shrugged away from him. He looked helplessly at me but said nothing.

Soon Emily wiped her nose and looked at me. Her eyes were slightly red and watery. "I just want a little sympathy, a little understanding."

I took a different tack. "How often do you have your time with your friends?"

"Tuesday night we go bowling. I've invited Emily to come but she doesn't want to."

"You know I don't like those guys; they're crude," Emily replied, "I don't fit in."

"Do any of the other wives or girlfriends go?" I asked.

"Yes. There are usually three or four of them there every Tuesday. They call themselves our cheerleaders."

"I for sure don't like those women," Emily said. "They aren't my kind of friends. We have nothing in common."

"But it isn't just Tuesday nights that you go out," Emily continued, "You are always going over to Billy's house on Saturdays for something or other."

"Billy is my brother," Dean explained, "And I don't go over there every Saturday. We like to watch college football sometimes or sometimes he needs help on his car. We just like hanging out together."

"And what can I do when you go off like that? I'm stuck at home with Ginger. We have to wait until you come back if we want to go anywhere."

"You only have one car?" I asked.

"Yes," Emily answered, "And besides, I can't drive."

"You don't drive?" I asked incredulously.

I learned that Emily had never learned to drive. She had several people offer to teach her and Dean had even paid for lessons, but she never took them.

"So that leaves you dependent on Dean for almost everything," I said.

"Or her brother or her mother or her sister, but mostly me," Dean added.

"I don't mind," Emily said.

"You said you don't mind but you complained that you are "stuck at home," didn't you?" I asked.

"That isn't the point," she said, "Dean could show a little consideration and spend some time with Ginger and me."

"Do you have any time away from Dean and your daughter," I asked.

"Just at work or when my family comes over."

"Dean, how are you feeling about this situation?" I asked.

Dean said, "I am sympathetic and maybe I should cut out some of my visits to Billy and after leagues are over, I can stay home on Tuesdays."

"I used to be a scout leader," Dean went on, "but that took up another evening and more weekends. I cut those out because Emily got so depressed when I was gone. I can't blame her. A child is not much company for an adult after a while. I guess I was pretty insensitive to her needs at that time. I'm trying but sometimes I just want to get away. Then I feel guilty about leaving her home alone."

It is pretty obvious that Emily was controlling Dean with her helplessness. I learned that he was the one who took their daughter to the doctor and to special school events. Sometimes, Emily would join him but she always could rely on the fact that she could not drive to put Dean in charge of all events requiring dealing with the world.

Emily was the youngest in her family and her brother and sister along with her parents had babied her. They taught her the dependent role and she had no other to fall back on. She had learned to not be strong or independent and she had little else with which to cope. When I addressed this issue with her in an individual session she denied it so strongly that I knew I had hit the nail on the head. But she wouldn't deal with it. She was unwilling to let go of the techniques of weakness that had been so successful in the past.

Dean was not perfect but he vacillated between trying to please Emily and trying to save his independence. At last, he left her. The last I heard, Emily was unmarried, still couldn't drive and was living with her parents. I am sure they commiserated with her for having been dumped by this cad. They have joint custody of their daughter but she lives with her father.

Comments

Learning how to cope with the world is something all parents must teach their children. When they teach them to use their dependence to do it they are just setting up the child for future unhappiness.

To learn a role is one thing, to maintain it is another. Dean continued to spoil Emily for a while. He wanted to do so because it made him feel powerful. It felt good at first to have her dependent on him. But after a while he realized that he needed a life too. Like every animal, when someone or something tries to control them, they begin to rebel. This is a basic animal instinct and it is a healthy one.

While I used an example of woman who used weakness to control, I have seen as many men as women who use weakness as a means of getting their way without regard for the other persons needs and rights.

If you are controlling through weakness, you need to face that fact and, as they say, get a life! Just because you are independent does not mean you can't enjoy a mutual interdependence that goes with love. Love requires two mature people making a commitment while not selling their souls.

Mr. Fixit

Let me tell one on myself. I had a nice couple come to see me. I cannot even remember what the problems were but we were at the last session, just wrapping up.

"I was so mad at you and Don I could just about spit," Ginny said with her South Carolina accent.

Don and I looked at each other. I was thinking that I thought I had remained neutral in this counseling. I was curious as to how I had flubbed up. "What did we do?" I asked.

"Remember last week when I told you I was starting to look for work?"

"Yes," I said.

"Well, you too started telling me about writing resumes and interview and the like."

"We were trying to offer suggestions," Don said.

"Well, you all didn't have to offer me suggestions because I know how I want to do it and I think I'm pretty good at finding jobs. You two acted like a couple of know-it-alls offering the dumb little gal some help."

"Uh-oh," I said. "I'm sorry we gave that impression."

"I don't get it. We were just trying to be helpful. We didn't want to put you down, did we?" Don said to me.

"We had good intentions but the message Ginny received was that she needed our help. We were acting superior in her eyes and that meant that she was being told that she was inferior."

"I see," Don said, "and even a counselor can goof up occasionally. I apologize, Ginny, I'll watch myself from now on."

"And you watch yourself, Mr. Counselor!" Ginny said, teasing me.

Well, I have watched myself and I try to watch not just what I say but how it might be received.

In this case, I had missed why Ginny was was telling us about her job search. She didn't want suggestions or lectured; she just wanted us to share what she was going through. What Don and I did was say to her that we don't care to just listen to you we are going to apply solutions. She was in a sharing mode we misunderstood and went into our (superior) helpful mode.

Some generalizations

Women and men often screw up in this basic area. Women do not realize that within every man there is a "Mr. Fixit" who wants to take some things they say and turn them into problems he can solve. Men need to recognize that women often want them to listen and share and that not every problem they talk about is a request for assistance.

It would help if women would signal when they are asking for help and would help if men would not be so quick to jump in and shatter conversations with solutions.

But it works the other way, too. Men do not usually like to be told what to do or how to do it by their partners. It is that male pride thing, I suppose. In fact, men don't like to ask for help whereas women are usually more willing to do so. When a man asks for help he feels like he is taking an inferior position in relationship to the helper.

Women usually see conversation as connection and security. That is one of the reasons that women like to talk to their partners. When their partners do not listen, they feel abandoned and insecure. This is especially true when there is a problem confronting them. Men tend to pull back and get silent while women want to feel secure by talking. Nothing could be more frustrating to both.

Charlotte and Jeff came to me with this exact problem. They had been married for ten years and had four children. They were both good parents but their marriage was almost dead. There were not many arguments, they still did family things and there was no drinking or other addictions or infidelities—just dull, drab co-existence.

"He won't talk," Charlotte began, "Even when our daughter was sick with pneumonia Jeff just sat there while I was in hysterics."

Jeff just sat there, his hands in his lap and his long legs crossed out in front of him. He showed no emotion.

"We used to talk all the time," Charlotte continued, "Then one day I woke up and realized we hadn't had a conversation in over a year."

"Oh, I think we did," Jeff said.

"He speaks!" Charlotte interjected.

"You remember any conversations, Jeff?" I asked.

"Well, not specifically, but I think we had a talk or two."

"I know and you are wrong. He's wrong. He lets me rattle on and he just sits there looking dumb and happy. He shows me nothing. I can't tell what he's thinking and what he's feeling—if he has any feelings! I would never know if he feels anything. Sometimes I think I'm going crazy. He won't argue, he won't complain, he won't even tell me a joke. He says nothing and I feel like I'd be better off with a dog, at least a dog can show you some feeling."

"What do you say, Jeff, she's said quite a lot about you? Any comments?"

"I guess she's right. I just don't know what to say. I know that disappoints her."

"Jeff, that's a beginning. You expressed a lot."

Jeff smiled.

"I never heard him say that much about anything important before," Charlotte said, "See if you can get some more out of him. Betcha can't."

Jeff looked down at his shoes.

Jeff and Charlotte could not see what was happening but I could. Charlotte was bitter about Jeff's lack of communication and when he did attempt to communicate she inadvertently punished him for trying. When he was punished like that, Jeff was confused. He did not want to strike back because he thought that would only make matters worse. His strategy, which did not work, was just to shut up, to withdraw from further communication.

Charlotte was probably always more vocal that Jeff. He could not keep up with her when it came to talk so he gradually quit trying. The less he talked the more she tried to pressure him to do so. The more he was pressured the further he withdrew, and so on.

When people are in a situation where they are "damned if they do and damned if they don't" they are suffering from what the psychologists call, "learned helplessness." They become dull and inexpressive. They soon quit expressing things to themselves and they do not honestly know what they feel and think.

Jeff was in that situation. He no longer recognized his own feelings. He did communicate with his co-workers but when he got home, he went into his "dumb mode" as he called it.

The solution for Jeff and Charlotte was for him to practice talking—talking about anything—while she listened. She became aware of how she was punishing his efforts and managed to get that under control.

A year after our final session of marriage counseling, they did return. I was happy to learn that they were continuing to communicate. This time they returned to get some suggestions on child management. They worked hard and I think they will do just fine.

Lisa and John
Power Imbalance

There was a message in the way they came to my office. John swaggered behind his wife and me, looking indifferent to this whole process. I could tell he was not involved in this process and that he was there as a favor to her. In the office, he chose the chair next to the window and proceeded to check out the view.

Lisa began to tell me that their relationship was in trouble. "I have never loved anyone else. I want to be happy with him and I don't think he is trying."

"Why's that?" I asked.

"Well, I am the one who does everything. I cook, I do the laundry, I do the cleaning and I do the grocery shopping. He just comes home whenever the mood hits him and expects to be waited on. And I have a full-time job, too."

"We have a child and are expecting another and he shows no interest in the family thing. He leaves all the baby stuff up to me. He won't play with the baby or give her a bath and god forbid that she should have a messy diaper!"

She went on, "He comes and goes when he wants to and he doesn't do anything around the house. He only says he loves me when he wants sex."

"Does it work?" I asked.

"Well, yes," she said, "I gotta accept his attention when I can get it."

I turned to John. "We are talking about you as if you aren't here. What do you have to say?"

Without interrupting his study of the view from my office, he said, "I'm listening."

"See what I mean, he doesn't care." Then turning toward him she said, "Johnny, please talk to the man; please try for me and your baby!"

"What do you want me to say? You've said it all."

"Johnny, pleeeze!" she cried.

I asked Lisa to be quiet while I talked to John. "It seems like you don't really care about this relationship; is that true?"

"Nah, I like her," John said looking in my direction.

"Do you love her?"

"I guess so."

"How do you show it to her?"

"Show what?" John replied.

"How do you show her you love her?"

"I tell her," he said.

"Yeah, when you want me in bed!" Lisa interrupted.

"Whatever." John shrugged and turned back to the window.

"John, do you want to stay in this relationship?" I asked.

"Yeah, it's nice."

"Sure it's nice for you," Lisa said, "You get to be treated like a damned king and I have to be your slave girl! I do all the work and you just sit around waiting to be waited on and there's hell to pay if our daughter demands any of my time when you want a beer! What's in it for me? What's in it for me? Answer me, Johnny, what's in it for me?"

"You get me," John answered with a smirk on his face.

At this point I separated them and while Lisa returned to the waiting room I continued with John. John remained non-committal about the whole thing. He told me that living together and having a baby was her idea. The only thing he wanted was for her to quit nagging him. He was honest about saying that he was quite comfortable with things as they were and he felt no compulsion to do any of the chores and he added that he was not "cut out to be a father."

I met with Lisa next and she was red-eyed with tears. She was very emotional and my efforts to calm her down were only partially successful. She kept asking, "Can you help us?" and she did not seem to want an answer. I finally told her that I had very little hope for this relationship but if she wanted things to change, she had to do something drastic to convince him of her seriousness. I said she needed to make him uncomfortable. She rejected that for fear that she would lose him.

I called John back in and we resumed a couple session.

This is what I told them: "My assessment of this situation is that the relationship is entirely one-sided and that makes this a very sick attempt at a relationship. There is sex but no shared passion. There is no romance.

"I believe that John has come to this session because Lisa wanted him to do so. John, you have shown from the beginning that you are not interested in improving this relationship and I don't say that to put you down; I believe that is your honest position. You are comfortable with things as they are.

"Lisa, you need to understand that John is not really committed to this relationship—not like you are. You treat him—as you say—'like a king,' and why should the king want to change things. Kings never do. And you have made him king. You do not want to change that for fear that he would leave and as long as you keep him comfortable like that he will put up with your complaints.

"You two have a dysfunctional relationship. Not only is it dysfunctional, it isn't likely to change. I see no reason for you to continue in relationship counseling."

With that, John got up and started for the door. He shook my hand and thanked me, much to my surprise.

But Lisa started pleading with me to see them again. Before John got completely out the door, I told them that I would see them again if John ever decided to make more of a commitment to try.

I offered to see Lisa again individually but assured her that working on this relationship was futile at this point. She was not happy with this and finally left the room.

Comments:

This relationship illustrates the problems that occur when power in the relationship gets out of balance. I know that a many people believe that a love relationship should never have an issue of power but it is always there. It only becomes obvious when the balance is tilted drastically as in this case.

When one person wants something the other has control over then the second person has power over the first. If I want to buy your car and you want to sell it, the distribution of power could be equal, more on your side or more on mine. If you are desperate for money then I might have upper hand and get you to come down or add some other items to the deal. If I really crave that car then you have the power and you can get more money out of me. If it is equal then we will probably try to tilt the balance one way or the other. That is the fun of haggling.

In the case of John and Lisa, John had the power. Lisa wanted to have a happy marriage and family and she wanted John to join her in that. Unfortunately for Lisa, John felt no need to change. He liked the balance of power the way it was. John had the power because Lisa wanted much from him and he did not want anything different from her.

The solution in cases where the balance of power is out of whack is for the person who has less power to do something to shift it back. How is that done? Check the next case.

Kurt and Olivia
My Way or the Hiway

Every now and then a couple comes for help with their marital problems and it quickly becomes apparent that there is no help for them as a couple. Kurt and Olivia had that kind of marriage, but it was not apparent at first.

Kurt was sent to me for anger management. His wife and son were in a shelter for abused women and their children. The court had ordered him to get counseling for his anger and to follow that up with marriage counseling if his wife decided to return to him.

Kurt was also very elusive when I asked him about the abuse. He kept saying that was not important or that the sheriff and the county attorney had exaggerated everything. He said his lawyer told him to plead guilty or he would end up in prison so he did.

I proceeded to lead Kurt through the educational material on anger. He was polite but I did not think that I was getting through to him. He would take the handouts and leave my office at the end of the session and one time I found some them blowing across the parking lot when I went home.

I gave Kurt some assignments and he would never give me a straight answer when I asked how the assignments went. All he would do is say he would be a "new man" when Olivia came back. I decided that Olivia's contribution to the anger management treatment would be very valuable. I, too, looked forward to seeing Olivia.

Olivia did come. I was quite surprised at her looks. Kurt was a short, rough looking man who was not articulate. He peppered his conversation with obscenities. Olivia was a tall, attractive woman who obviously cared about her looks and spoke very intelligently. The contrast was about as extreme as it could be.

But as we proceeded into the first couple session I began to see other aspects of the relationship. When I asked about the abuse, Olivia looked at Kurt and his brow tightened. She then turned to me and said, "Oh, it wasn't much, just a shove."

I realized then that Olivia had submitted to Kurt and that she was not about to say anything he would not like. They were in collusion to protect Kurt from facing the consequences of his behavior. I decided to see Olivia alone for a few minutes. Kurt was not happy about that. I assured him that this was not uncommon in marital counseling and he finally left.

"Olivia, I want to know if you are afraid of Kurt," I said.

"No, I'm not," she said.

"Olivia, you spent two months in a shelter and the court found sufficient reason to charge him. I think you are not being honest."

She was quiet for a moment and then said, with tears in her eyes, "Between you and me, confidentially?"

"Yes."

Then she told me that he had pushed her but he did it with such force that she was knocked off their front steps and onto the gravel driveway. "And he never said he was sorry. He blamed me for making him mad."

She went on to describe a life of what I would call tyranny by her husband. He would never admit to making any mistakes and he would never listen to her ideas. It was not surprising that he didn't apologize when he knocked her to the ground but it did make me think about their relationship.

I asked her why she came back and she said that Kurt had told her that he was taking anger management and he was a "new man." He also promised that they would have marital counseling which he had refused for years.

"You know, he really does love me and he is so good to Jason (their one year old daughter). He just needs a little help."

I told her that I did not hold out much hope but she urged me to try to help them. I agreed.

I invited Kurt back into the room and began to talk to them about goals. They agreed to spend some time together each week. I told them that we would continue to work on forming goals for their relationship.

They did spend time together and it went very well. Olivia had not moved back in at the first couple's session but she decided to do so after having such a wonderful time talking with her husband.

"He actually listened to me and he even apologized for treating me so badly," she said.

That session went well but I still had the feeling that Kurt was not being completely honest.

Olivia called in to cancel the next session. She said that Kurt had to work late. The same thing happened the next week.

They finally came in after about a month. This time I was startled at how Olivia had changed. Her hair was messy and she was wearing some ill-fitting jeans and a sweatshirt with stains on it. Kurt was the same. They looked better matched now.

I asked how things were going.

Kurt said, "Fine," but Olivia said, "Could be better."

I asked for clarification.

"Kurt still has problems with his anger. He got upset when I didn't get up in time to get his coffee made last week."

I asked Kurt for his version.

"She knows I am short-tempered in the morning. She knew that I would be pissed off if she didn't get my coffee ready but she slept in anyhow. I work hard everyday and it isn't too much to ask for her to show a little consideration."

"You think she slept late on purpose?" (I decided to hold myself back on the obvious male chauvinism implied in Kurt's statement.)

"Makes you wonder when all she does is lay around all day."

Olivia glanced at Kurt and then at the floor. "Sorry I brought that up," she said.

"Kurt, you seem to be saying that Olivia plots to make you angry. Is that right?"

"She just doesn't think. She just thinks of herself. I have to treat her like a kid. She has plenty of book-learning but sometimes she doesn't have the sense that God gave a goose."

"You are pretty hard on her," I commented.

"I wouldn't be if she would just think. Not just about the coffee, she just refuses to see things from my point of view about anything," Kurt said.

"Is it possible that she does think but she doesn't think your way? Her point of view might be as valid as yours."

"He says it's his way or the hiway," Olivia said.

"You don't really mean that, do you, Kurt?" I asked.

"I do. It's my house; I pay the rent. I bring in the most money and I bought the furniture and my money pays most of the bills. In my house it's my way or the hiway!"

"See?" Olivia said.

"Either get used to it or hit the road!" Kurt said to Olivia.

I turned to Kurt to interrupt but he beat me to it and interrupted me.

"I think we've had enough of this marriage counseling stuff. The solution to our problem is simple; either she shapes up or she ships out. Let's go, woman!" With that he walked out of the office and Olivia trailed behind him like an obedient puppy.

"Olivia…" I started. She turned to me and shrugged her shoulders. She pretended to smile.

The next day I called Olivia at home to see if she was OK. She said that Kurt hadn't been physically violent to her but he continued to lecture her "…and stuff." I asked what stuff she was referring to. She said, "Oh, just little things."

"Like what?

There was a moment of silence and her voice returned with tears. "He threw my parakeet outside. And it is freezing out there. I don't know what happened to Peedie; he wouldn't let me out to look for him."

Olivia continued to cry on the phone, interjecting apologies in between sobs. When she had regained some composure, she told me stories of abuse that she had told no one. She had been physically abused and she had suffered forced sex from him. He had a pattern of calling her stupid and accused her of having affairs.

I told Olivia that I thought Kurt was dangerous. He was capable of doing more damage to her and perhaps to her daughter. I didn't see Kurt as capable of using counseling. I told her that she should return to the shelter.

Olivia said she did not want to give up on their marriage. She said that maybe another counselor would have more luck with him (he had told her he would never come back to see me).

I told Olivia that it was his way "or the hiway," and with that attitude, he was never going to change. I again urged her to seek counseling for herself and to go to the shelter. She said she would think about it.

Why women stay

One of the questions that keeps coming up is why abused women do not leave their abusive husbands. The most common answer I have heard is that they do not have the earning potential to make it without their husbands. This is often true. I can recall back in my dark days as a public assistance worker meeting with a woman who had had it with her abusive husband. She wanted out and hoped that getting Aid to Families with Dependent Children (ADC in those days) would support her when she left him. When I told her how much she and her three children would get on ADC she said to me very bitterly, "I guess I'll just have to learn to outrun him."

I felt sorry for this woman but could offer no help. However, as I began doing counseling I saw another side. Some women do not leave because of their dream of having a family. They still hope that somehow the violence will stop. Many women hang on to the obviously mistaken belief that if they just keep loving the guy he'll just have to change.

Another thing that is often overlooked is that in most cases over half the time the man isn't too bad. In fact, he can be quite nice. Moreover, he can be very repentant over the times when he "loses it All of this is very encouraging to the woman's dream of a happy relationship.

Kurt was a different sort of guy. He could never admit that he was wrong and needed to change. His abuse was totally justified in his mind.

Postscript

Olivia did finally take the hiway option. After that, I heard that Kurt took a different hiway to another state. I sincerely hope she is doing well.

Marla and Chuck
Lured into Counseling

Marla called more than once before she came in. Here message was always the same, "I don't think it will do any good for me to come in by myself and I already asked and he refused." I urged her to come in anyway. Finally, she did.

Marla was a pleasant woman in her mid-forties. She had been a teacher in a rural school for many years. Her husband, Chuck, was a truck driver. The last of their three sons had moved on to his own life a year before.

She began crying almost immediately. I handed her a tissue. She excused herself as she regained composure and said, "I'm sorry, I promised myself I wouldn't do that."

She told me the story of her marriage to Chuck. "You know, he was never a real romantic type, but I thought he would change. After the kids came along he seemed to divide his time between work and TV. The boys and I just weren't part of his life except when he would yell at us. You know, we haven't even had sex in over five years. Do you know how that makes me feel?"

"I started talking about seeing a counselor about ten years ago. I would tell him I was unhappy and he would—you know what he would tell me?"

I thought I knew but I signaled her to continue.

"He would tell me that maybe I should go to a shrink because there wasn't anything wrong with him." (Just as I suspected.)

"Lately, he makes fun of any mention of counseling. He says things like, 'Only a nut would tell everything to a shrink'—he always calls counselors that. When I mentioned I was coming to see you he started cussing and swearing and stomped out of the house."

"I guess he's pretty insecure with this, isn't he?"

"I never thought of it that way," she said.

"People who object to anything that strongly must feel a lot," I said. "Anyhow, you're here and that's a beginning."

"Yes, I'm here but what good will that do? I know I'm not perfect but I'm not here for just myself, I'm here for our marriage."

"I know that it is commonly believed that one party can't do anything when two parties are involved, but that is only partly true. I'll explain to you what you can do if you like."

"I guess I'm a little skeptical," she said, "but I'm desperate, I'll try anything if you think it will work."

I told her that she was letting him have all the power and that he was quite comfortable the way he was. I asked her to tell me if that was not the case.

"I don't know—maybe."

"For instance, what do you do to try to please him?"

"I always have a hot meal on the table for him when he gets home. Sometimes, he is late, so I warm it up for him."

"What else?" I asked.

"He likes to watch TV and I usually sit down by him and watch with him, even though I don't care for the shows he likes to watch. In fact, I used to read but I gave that up because he objected."

"Anything else you've given up for him?"

"My friend, Abbie, and I used to take walks in the evening but he criticized that because he didn't like her. He said he was afraid she was putting ideas in my head. She's divorced, you know."

"Well, Marla, you have made a lot of sacrifices for him. Now, ask yourself, has it worked? Did it get you anything you wanted?"

She thought for a minute and said, "No, I guess not."

"I suggest this, then, quit sacrificing for him."

"That might be hard. I guess I'm used to mothering people, even my husband. Don't you think he might get even madder if I do that?"

"He will if you do it in a rebellious way. All I am suggesting is that you start taking care of yourself; doing what you want while really taking nothing from him. You see, you have given him a lot of power. He could not take it if you hadn't given it to him. As long as he feels comfortable that his wife is thoroughly under his control, he will not want to change.

"Start tonight. Make your supper, enough for both of you, and if he isn't there, put his in the refrigerator and when he gets home, tell him where it is."

"What if he objects? He'll probably be mad."

"Just calmly tell him that you would be glad to heat it up for him if that's what he wants. You see, you are depriving him of nothing. You're even willing to accommodate him if he asks. What can he do? He would probably feel foolish to demand any more."

"I guess I can try," she said.

"And I want you to stop at a book store on your way home and pick out a book you would like to read. And I want you to start reading it tonight."

"He won't like that."

"What do you have to lose? I think you have sacrificed for too many years for nothing. You need to take some of your life back and in doing that you will be taking back some of the power that is yours."

Marla tried what I suggested but I did not know that for several months. Then one day I got a call from her. She said that Chuck wants to see me. I suggested they both come and set an appointment.

When the day came, Chuck and Marla came into my office and sat down. I asked, "How may I help you?"

Chuck was more vocal than I had expected. He explained that he and Marla had been living an unhappy marriage for too many years. He said he was sick of it and he was also afraid that he was going to lose his wife.

I hid my amazement and glanced at Marla who was holding back a grin.

We negotiated a few issues with amazing ease. Chuck wanted a few changes and was willing to make some concessions to Marla. At the end of the session Chuck said, "We'll try what you suggested and if we need further help, we'll call." I knew that he wanted to retain some control and I respected that. What he had said assured me that he would put effort into making a happy marriage. The battle was mostly over before they reached my office.

Comments

Of course, there were many problems in the marriage of Chuck and Marla but there were many strengths. Parenthetically, I do not believe a counselor has to solve everything and having some faith in people's strengths usually pays off.

You cannot blame Chuck for all of this problem because Marla had given away her power in the relationship. However, you cannot blame her, either. Marla was sacrificing her power in hopes that it would gain her the happy marriage she desired.

What happens in these cases is that the one who gets the power begins to accept it as the way things are and feels that there is no need to change. Although Chuck did not feel entirely happy in the relationship he didn't know why. He accepted his position of power and let Marla spoil him but he knew, deep down, that things could be better.

Marla started moving the center of power when she went ahead and kept her appointment with me against his explicit wishes. She further kept moving it when she followed my suggestions. She was taking back her life and her power but she was not taking away anything from Chuck.

Could it have turned out differently? Yes. If Chuck had no motivation to continue the marriage he could have ignored the things she was doing or even taken them as an excuse to end the marriage. However,

Marla and I agreed that it was worth the gamble to make the marriage better. After all, she had nothing to lose.

Chuck is like many people who find themselves in the power seat. When the power starts shifting back to the center they wake up and start thinking about what they had taken for granted. Chuck, like a lot of men, is uncomfortable with relationship dynamics. He could not understand what was wrong and he avoided it. He felt threatened by any attempt that Marla made to talk about the relationship. After all, who wants to contend in an area where they do not feel competent? In addition, men do not like to go to an "expert" who will probably tell them that they are ignorant, stupid or just plain mean. They do not know that ethical counselors do not try to belittle their clients. Besides, most men are "Mr. Fixits" who don't want to call for help. They may not actually fix it, whether it is the washing machine or the relationship, but they sure do not want someone else to do it.

Michelle and David
Psychobabble Domination

He was tall and slender and he looked the part of the rancher he was. He had brown hair and a thick mustache. He had rough hands and a firm grip yet he seemed gentle and a little shy.

"Well, what brings you here?" I asked.

"Wahl, Mikki said I should come?" he said.

"Why?"

"Not shore."

I decided to get a little background. Michelle and David were dating and occasionally living together. They had known each other since high school and they had been romantically involved for the past three years. They had no children.

He told me that Mikki had been involved in therapy in another agency and that she wanted him to get into therapy, too. She told him that he should find a male therapist to work with and that is how he happened to choose to come to me.

David told me that she had insisted that they were not getting along because of his "issues."

I asked him to explain.

"Ahh don't really know, she just said I had some issues and if I don't deal with them she is out of here."

He did explain that they didn't get along very well since she started her therapy. "Ahh don't know what that counselor is telling her but it sure has her riled up."

I told him that there is probably a lot more to this than he or I know at this point and we need Michelle to come in and help us get started.

Two weeks later, David came with Michelle. She was an attractive woman with long blonde hair. She was as verbal as David was non-verbal.

I told her that David and I had met and he was willing to continue with me but I felt that we needed to see things from her point of view in order to continue.

"David is a classic case of co-dependency. He grew up in an alcoholic home and his father was abusive and controlling."

"Wait a minute," David interrupted, "My Dad never abused me and my parents were both social drinkers and not alcoholic."

"See what I mean," Michelle said looking at me, "he's in denial. He can't see anything wrong with his parents. When I bring it up, he gets defensive. Obviously (she turned to him) you're refusing to deal with these issues and we can't go on like that."

"How has his family background affected your relationship?" I asked.

"He won't talk about feelings; his feelings are all bottled up. He denies problems, uses every kind of defense mechanism and refuses to recognize them. Since I have been in therapy I realize how sick our relationship has become and we can't build a relationship until we both deal with our issues."

"Do you mind my asking why you have concluded that he grew up in an alcoholic family and that his father abused him?" I asked.

"You don't have to be a skid row bum to be an alcoholic. His parents can't make it through the day without some kind of alcohol. Their social life consists of drinking buddies at the local bowling alley.

As for the abuse, if you just met his father you would see. That man can't carry on a conversation; he just lectures and dictates. He is domineering and puts down David at every opportunity."

"Yah, but they don't drink all the time. Ahh ain't never seen them drunk. And Dad likes to argue. He's all blow and no show. He never hit any of us kids. Shore, he puts me down sometimes, but he also apologizes for it. He's a good man."

"Denial and co-dependency, right?" she looked at me.

I did not agree that this is a case of co-dependency, one of those catch-all categories that is too general to be helpful. When people use that term they need to define what is meant or it is meaningless.

As I explored this relationship further I discovered that Michelle went into therapy because she felt that David was controlling their relationship. The therapist she was seeing was a lady who had minimum credentials and experience in the treatment of substance abuse. She was limited by her experience and training.

Therapists can only function with the information and point of view they are given. Despite our desire for it to be different, we therapy-types are not able to read minds. We might be able to make some good guesses but that is all we can do, make educated guesses. Michelle's therapist got Michelle's point of view and her view of the facts.

Michelle was impressed with what she had learned from her therapist. But she went further. With less knowledge and experience than her therapist, she used what she had learned to turn the tables on David. She knew something he did not know and she used that to tilt the power scales in her favor. He did not know anything about psychology so she had the upper hand.

(Please note, I am not criticizing the recovery or twelve step programs as such. I am criticizing the use of psychology, whether it comes from sophomore psych course or a TV guru, to dominate a spouse, friend or any body. It is a tool and not a weapon. You cannot psychologize your partner.)

She accused him of being in denial. So what defense could he use? If he agreed with her he betrayed his parents; if he argued he was "in denial." He could not win.

Therapists and counselors cringe when they find that they have a pseudo-psychologist in that other chair. In addition, when they bring or send their partners or children to get fixed we cringe and shudder to the depths of our souls. We know that we have someone who is on a power and superiority trip and they are very hard to deal with. To challenge them is to challenge the credibility of their previous guru and the current therapist usually comes off the loser.

Michelle's therapist not only gave her knowledge she gave her power and superiority over David. David was squirming like a man in some horror movie who has been sentenced to death and does not even know what he did wrong.

So, what happened to David and Michelle? They split up. Michelle would not come to couple counseling because "I have to deal with my own issues and David has to deal with his." David and I could not find those "issues" he was supposed to work on so he chose not to continue in therapy and to just give up on the relationship. The last I heard he had found a new girlfriend.

Rocky and Shelly
For Love or Money

They called him, "Rocky." He looked like a body builder, although he said he hadn't worked out in two years. Shelly, his wife, was a tall slender woman with black curly hair. Both were in their mid twenties and well dressed. Rocky worked as a salesman for an investment corporation. Shelly was a Certified Public Accountant. They had one child, a two-year-old daughter. Her mother provided day care for them.

Although they had a better than average income, their problems are similar to those of other couples with less income. I have found that problems are much the same across all income and education levels, races and religions.

Shelly began, "I don't want to continue this way. We aren't a family or a couple anymore we are just people who share a dwelling. I want a marriage and a family or I want to end it."

"Look, Shelly, we've been over this a dozen times. We have what a lot of families don't have, we have a secure future. There aren't many people who can say that. What about your parents? They just live from check to check. If we don't build a sound financial base we will have nothing; we'll be just like them."

"Don't bring my parents into this. At least they are happy and they love each other. I want to have a marriage I can enjoy, not just a business arrangement. Marriage isn't a firm, it's a lot more than that!"

"It might be a lot more than just money but it would be nothing at all without money. Can't you see that?"

"Wait a minute," I interrupted, "I'm sure you've had this argument many times and you haven't resolved it. I am also certain that you would both like to save this marriage or I would only be talking to one of you, or neither.

"Rocky, I get the impression that you are focused on the financial and security aspects of marriage. Do I have that right?" I asked.

"Yes, that's right."

"And, Shelly, you have alluded to other aspects of marriage. I would like you to elaborate so I can understand it. Just talk to me, not Rocky, OK?"

"I know money is important. I would just like to have some time for our marriage; time together. You know, I just want us to have fun. I want Rocky to take some time off and we can do something. I'd like a nice leisurely meal together, maybe some dancing or a movie. I'd like to have sex that didn't seem like it was an obligation. I'd like him to kiss and hug me and just ask me to take a walk. And I'd like for him to stay home one night and get to know Eleni. He could give her a bath or read or a story or something."

"And we all go to the poor house as a family, I suppose. Is that part of your dream, too? Get real, Shelly!" Rocky interrupted.

"Hold it, Rocky," I said, let Shelly finish.

"That was about all I had to say," Shelly said.

"Rocky and Shelly, can't you reach a compromise on this? Money is necessary, of course. I don't think there is any argument about it. And I don't think Rocky believes that marriage is only a business proposition. I that right, Rocky?"

"Of, course, but you can't have the romantic stuff unless you have the security as a foundation. Just see how long the romance lasts when the repossess your house and throw you on the street!"

"You mean I have to wait until we reach some point when we have enough financial security before we can really be married? Just when will that be, Rocky; just when? Will two million be close? How about five million? Maybe we have to reach a billion before Rocky will say, 'OK, now let's get busy with the romantic stuff.' Is that right, Rocky. Tell me. Tell me now."

Rocky said, "Shelly, quit being a smart ass."

"Rocky you're correct in wanting financial security but what good will it do to have a sound financial base if your marriage falls apart?" I asked.

"I never thought a counselor would take one person's side over the other," Rocky said, "I thought you were supposed to be neutral."

"Rocky, would you answer that question for me? Don't you think you should also be working on the marriage as you work for fiscal security?"

"In my opinion, I have to work hard while I'm young. That's what youth is for. When I'm forty I will be able to lay back and take it easy. Then we can go where we want and do what we want."

At this point, a cell phone rang. Rocky reached into his pocket, flipped it open and started talking to someone about business. "I gotta go," he said, "Look, I thank you for your efforts but this is getting us no place. I'm too busy to continue this. Thank you." With that, he walked out the door.

Shelly sat there. She grabbed a tissue and patted her eyes. "You see. He's not going to budge on this. He is obsessed with money, as you can see. I want more out of life than a portfolio of blue chips. I want to be loved and I want to love. It isn't going to happen for me in this marriage."

Shelly left Rocky when he refused to come back to counseling. I wish it had been different because Rocky was not a bad guy. He was an insecure guy. Shelly told me that his father was just like him and he was always trying to measure up. The strange thing was that Rocky's father had died of a heart attack at work when Rocky was 12. Shelly feared the same thing would happen to him.

Shelly got on with her life and after a heated divorce (over money and property), she finally remarried and had another child. I suppose Rocky is still being Rocky.

I tried to relate to Rocky but he did not relate. I do not think he knew how. I've seen that before, mostly with men. Men and women are raised differently. Little boys play with things and little girls use things to play with relationships. By the time they have grown up men are ill equipped to deal with relationships and are often more comfortable dealing with things. People are always more comfortable dealing with what they are used to and avoiding things with which they are less familiar.

Rocky was that way. He was comfortable with making money, something he was good at and something he could manipulate. He avoided relating to his wife and daughter because, I think, he felt less than competent relating on an emotional level. His wife was good at it. He turned it over to her and went on to do what he knew he was good at.

Men who have this deficiency need the patience and help of their partners. Unfortunately, men like Rocky are too insecure to admit that they need the help.

We tend to take skills like this for granted. It takes courage to admit that we need some help to enhance our relationship skills. Rocky could relate to clients and to others as he needed so he wasn't totally devoid of the ability to relate. With some help, I believe he could have got the hang of it.

Forgiveness
Patrick and Nanette.

Patrick was very upset. The first thing he said as he entered my office with his wife, Nanette in tow, was, "My finger is on the dial and I am ready to call the lawyer!"

He went on to explain that he had found that she was gambling. She had done that before and had gotten severely in debt. That was before they were married only a year ago. He had paid off her debt and made her promise that she would never gamble again. This time he had followed her after she got off work and she went to a casino bar across the state line. When she got home he asked her were she had been and she said that she worked late and then got out for coffee with her friends from work. He knew this was a lie and confronted her. That lead to a huge verbal fight and they went to bed that night in silence.

The next morning he gave her an ultimatum that she had to get help with her gambling problem and they were going to get into marriage counseling as soon as he could find a counselor.

Patrick and Nanette were both in their early forties. Neither had been married before and they had met at a singles club. Patrick was a maintenance supervisor at a local manufacturing company. He told me that he had been very frugal all his life and had a rather large nest egg.

Nanette was a day manager of a local restaurant. She told me that for her, money was for enjoyment as well as security. Over twenty years of working she had not accumulated any savings. She told me that she is not a "miser" like her husband.

Nanette had an appointment (made by her husband) for a gambling addiction assessment. She did not think that it was necessary. However, she did think that marriage counseling was necessary. I told her that I thought that both were called for.

"I didn't get married to have my savings eaten up with credit cards and gambling," Patrick began. "But ever since I have been with this woman she has been flushing my retirement down the drain with her irresponsible debts. I've paid her bills and bought her furniture and there is no end in sight."

"And I didn't think I was marrying a money grubbing miser who loves his money more than anything under God's blue sky. I didn't think I was getting hitched to a jackass who wants to act more like my father than my husband."

"You need more than a father, Nan, you need a keeper. You obviously can't be trusted to manage your own life so someone should do it for you," Patrick replied.

"OK," I interrupted, "Ok, lets get this under control. You are both angry at this moment and I can't blame either one of you. But blame isn't the issue. Blame leads to nothing good for your relationship."

"But, don't you see…" Patrick started.

"Let's take a time out from this argument, Patrick and Nanette, I want you to stop for a moment and think about what you want from this relationship. I want you to think in terms of what you want and not what you don't want."

They both stared at me for a moment.

"I've heard what you don't want," I said. Nanette doesn't want to be treated as if she is a child and Patrick doesn't want Nanette to use money irresponsibly. Now I want you to tell me what kind of relationship you do want. Nanette, can you begin?"

"I want us to have fun together. I want to go out together like we did before we got married."

"OK, now you, Patrick," I said.

"I guess I want to get us back to where we were, too. But I'm so danged worked up about this money thing and gambling that I'm having a hard time thinking positive. Sorry."

"That was honest of both of you," I said. "Now let's see if we can get at the bottom of some things. Patrick, would you be willing to back off on controlling Nan if it was a choice between that and the marriage?"

"I guess I don't see myself as controlling," Patrick began.

"Think back on what you have said about her needing a keeper. Doesn't that sound a bit like controlling?"

"I guess so, but...."

"I understand that you feel very anxious about this matter and I think there's some justification for it but control drives people away.

"Now, Nan, do you see that your use of money has severely threatened your relationship with Patrick. Would you be willing to make some changes here?"

"Yes. I just want us to get back to the way things were, like Patrick said."

"Nan, do you think gambling has caused a problem in your life?" I asked.

"I suppose it has. I just wanted some fun in my life and it wasn't happening at home."

"I'm glad you admitted that you have a problem with gambling and I think you ought to take that gambling assessment seriously. I know that no one wants to admit they have a problem with gambling but once you get past admitting the problem you are on your way to feeling good again."

"Do you think I should just forgive her for this and ignore the problem?" Patrick asked, still obviously upset.

"No, I don't. Nor do I think that she ought to forgive you right now for trying to control her. Neither of you need cheap forgiveness. Real forgiveness is necessary but in the case of two people who are intimately involved much depends on getting ready for forgiveness and doing it right."

Nanette went to her gambling assessment and she completed a treatment program. She continued in a support group for compulsive gamblers.

Patrick's addiction to control was much more difficult to overcome. His anxiety about it can be compared to how a person with a fear of heights would feel about letting go of the safety bar on a roller coaster. He could understand the harm his control was doing to the relationship but he could not seem to let go of the control.

What finally began to make him ease off was when I had Nanette produce a budget for her and Patrick. I had coached him ahead of time to consider what she had produced and give it a chance. He did. In fact, he liked the budget very much.

As usual, I had them spend special time together and they both liked leaving their problems behind and enjoying each other.

In our final session, I had them write letters to each other accepting responsibility for their behaviors and forgiving the other. They read them aloud in the session.

Comments

Patrick had begun to exercise control over finances from the beginning. He had grown up with a great fear of poverty and spending money was something he tried to avoid. Nanette had grown up in a family that treated money as something to enjoy. Her parents never worried about security. You can readily see that a clash was inevitable. Her attitude toward money and past debts raised Patrick's anxiety and control set in to lower it.

Nanette, feeling his control, began to seek relief from the stress created by Patrick's control by escaping into the excitement of gambling.

Dan and Rhonda
The Marital System

Dan called the agency where I work and asked for an appointment for him and his wife. I commented to the intake worker that it is not always a good sign when the man requests marital counseling. We set an appointment for Dan and his wife.

Dan and Rhonda came into my office and sat down. I noticed immediately that Rhonda pulled her chair a few inches away from Dan as she sat down. She kept her head down and would not make eye contact with me at first. She was a pretty woman, 29 years of age. Dan was a nice looking man of about the same age. They were high school sweethearts and married seven years before.

I asked them to tell me what had happened in their relationship.

"I thought everything was going just fine," Dan began, "and now she is behaving like a teen again."

I asked him to explain.

"Well, every night when I get home from work, she dresses up like a teenager and leaves. I have to cook supper for me and the kids and she doesn't come home until one or two in the morning. I think the kids and I are losing her."

"It isn't every night!" Rhonda interjected. Then she turned to me and said, "Don't you think that I deserve a night out with my friends every now and then? He has his softball buddies and does just the same. Can't I have fun, too?"

"I don't go out every night—and yes, Rhonda, you do go out almost every night. I go out once a week and I'm back by midnight. And I don't know why you have to dress like a slut."

"Slut! I'm not dressing like a slut, I'm just dressing up to feel good about myself," and turning to me she added, "I'm just hangin' with my girlfriends, I'm not looking for trouble."

"Yeah, you can't tell me that!" Dan said, and turning to me, "What would you think if you saw a woman dressed in tight jeans and a top so tight you can see her nipples?"

At this Rhonda folded her arms and turned away from both Dan and me.

"That's how she deals with it. I think it is over!" Dan said to me.

Rhonda snatched a tissue from the box on my desk.

I could see that this couple was not going to have a productive session as long as they stayed in the room together. Hostility was in the air. I had to separate them. I talked to Rhonda first and Dan returned to the waiting room.

"Well, Rhonda, I can see there is a lot more to this than I have heard up to now. Would you care to tell me how things look from your point of view?" I began.

"I don't know if I want to go on with this marriage," she said, "I'm getting tired of Dan always accusing me of being a whore and giving me the third degree every time I'm a little late coming home."

"Are you running away from him?

"No, not really," she began, "Well, maybe. Well, I do feel better when he isn't around. He's so negative about everything; he makes me feel like a, a…"

"Like a naughty little girl," I finished for her.

"Exactly. I feel like I'm always wrong, like I have to defend everything I do. Believe me, it's no fun."

"So what's it like when you go out?" I asked.

"I get to let my hair down; to be myself and have fun again" she said.

I invited her to go on.

"My friends treat me like I have a brain in my head. We can laugh and be silly if we want to and nobody questions you."

We talked on about her nights out. She told me that she and her friends drink and go to a particular bar where they play Country Western music. After a little probing she told me she has danced with one of the guys there. She added, "Dan and I haven't gone out to dance or anything in the last five years."

I checked my notes and suggested, "Since your first child was born?"

"Yes, I guess that's about when the marriage started going to hell."

This is a significant point in the marriage of about everyone. Couples seldom anticipate the impact of turning their dyad into a tryad. Once a child comes along, things change and I don't mean just diapers.

Some people doubt the maternal instinct but I think it is real. Many women don't realize until they have a child what it will do to their feelings and perspectives on life. For many it means they have become full-fledged adult females. They now belong to the world of their mothers, aunts and older sisters. They can feel their "familiness."

For others women, it is a new love affair, a cute, dependent little being all their own who will fill in that void of love that has never been satisfied.

For men the range of feelings run total confusion and indifference to a new-found sense of responsibility and love almost the same as the mother feels. For many, it takes a great deal of getting used to, this fatherhood thing.

No matter what the reactions, the whole marriage changes. You can't just decide to go somewhere on a whim because there are naps to contend with, diaper bags and other paraphernalia babies require. Then when you are ready to go out the door the little bundle of joy throws up and runs a fever. So much for "normal" life.

Too often, the spouses find themselves divided. They do not realize its happening at first but this truly blessed event has created a widening chasm between them. I might add, parenthetically, that it strikes me as odd that couples in marital trouble will often have another child in hopes that this will hold them together. I have never heard of that producing a happy marriage but I have seen much evidence of just the opposite.

A family is a system and that is what this chapter is about. Dan and Rhonda hadn't realized that their problems had started when the system changed. I do not want to go into needless details here about the system paradigm for understanding human behavior but I will point out of few of the principles involved.

For one thing, as I pointed out above, when a system changes, the impact on all members of that system changes at the same time. Going from couple to family is one of the most dramatic systemic changes you can imagine. If you have gone through that, you should reflect upon the adjustments you and your spouse had to make at that time.

Every system tries to maintain itself and members of that system will usually try hard to help the system maintain itself. Unfortunately, spouses will often go to the extreme. In the case of Rhonda and Dan, the more Rhonda tried to distance herself from Dan, the more he tried to hold the family together by giving her "the third degree" and trying to control her. The more he acted that way, the more she felt the need to get away.

"Oh, it's Rhonda's fault?" I hear you cry. To this I answer, "No." This is what they call, "linear reasoning." Linear reasoning goes like this: A causes B. If it is raining, the street gets wet. You would not say that wet streets cause rain. A causes B but B doesn't cause A. This is the common sense approach and it works most of the time, but when you are looking at living organisms this logic proves faulty.

Systems work on a different basis called a "feedback loop." The feedback loop model says that A influences B and B influences A. The logic of the feedback loop is that Rhonda's behavior is influenced by Dan's behavior and Dan's behavior is influenced by Rhonda's behavior. Dan complains because she leaves too often and she leaves too often because he complains.

I compare these interactions to a Ping-Pong game. As long as one keeps hitting the ball back the other will hit it back in turn. And so on. While the ball has a nasty twist to it, it will continue to be nasty as it goes back and forth. To change the nasty game someone has to do something different. Someone has to have the courage to let a nasty ball fly by and put down the paddle. Someone with that courage has to say, "I don't want to play a nasty game any more, I want to play a nice game with you; one that will bring us together.

So what extremely wise thing do I say to a couple like Rhonda and Dan? Do I require them to go through individual sessions to gain profound insight into their personality defects? Or do I harangue Rhonda, telling her she is no longer a teenager or turn on Dan and tell him to quit being such a nag? No, I tell them to have a date; a weekly date. Why?

I believe a new game is called for. I believe that they quit spending special time together and so quit meeting each other's relationship needs. But most of all, I believe a new, healthy interaction is needed, a new game to compete with the old, nasty one.

So, I tell them to have a date. I tell them to have a minimum of an hour together each week with no kids, no friends, no TV or other distraction. I tell them that during this hour nothing of a negative nature is to be discussed. I tell them that if all they do is spend the hour in silence, that's fine. I also tell them that they only have to do this "until death you do part." They already made such a promise so I do not think I'm asking too much.

If you are reading this, you are ready to apply it. Have a date. Take charge of it. Do not have the attitude that you will wait and see if your partner will initiate it; you do it!

Robin and Miles
Security vs. Excitement

Robin and Miles met each other in high school. He was from one of the wealthy farming families in the area. They had lived in that county since shortly before the Civil War. They had diversified investments and owned several agriculture-related businesses that helped them weather the ups and downs of the farm economy.

Miles had not been an athlete like his older brothers had been and he was only a mediocre student. He had tried various extracurricular activities but nothing seemed to work out. He was shy and awkward but easy to like. He seldom had a date and then it was only in the context of some school activity.

Robin and her family had moved into the area when she was a sophomore. Her father was a construction worker who worked for a company that moved him from one place to another for his jobs. He made enough money to take care of his wife and two children.

Robin was a good student but not an excellent one. She was in the marching band and the pep club. She gained some popularity although she was new to this small town. She described herself as "bubbly and full of excitement." Soon she was dating, "and breaking hearts right and left," as she said it.

She told me that she always liked Miles because he was "so sweet and kind," but she never dated him until the end of the senior year. "I had to pursue him," she told me, "he was to shy to pursue me. I had to ask him out—that's right—ask him out three times before he would go."

They were married shortly after they got out of high school. When I met them they had been married for 23 years. They had two children who were in college. Robin had started the counseling sessions by coming in by herself. She had said that she wanted to check some things out before Miles came in.

Robin was an attractive woman of 41. She told me that she was here to find out what was wrong with her. She said she had panicked when she was 39 and "facing that big 4-0." She had gained forty pounds during their marriage and decided that it had to come off. She said, "If I can't be 23 again, I'll at least do what I can to look it."

I asked what she meant by something being wrong with her.

"Well, I got all that weight off and got into clothes I hadn't worn for over 15 years. I bought new clothes. The kids and Miles were very complimentary. Everyone was complimentary. Then things got back to normal and the compliments gradually ceased. I decided to check out some strangers."

She started going to bars where younger people hung out and soon she found younger men paying attention to her.

"I met a guy called Carl. He was 25. He followed me around in one bar all night. I had to sneak out the back to get away from him. Then I saw him in another bar a couple of weeks later and he bought me a drink. We talked. I told him I was married. He said he didn't care if I didn't. That scared me. He insisted I take his phone number and I guess I did." She reached in her purse and pulled out a matchbook and handed it to me.

"I have taken that out of my purse a thousand times in the last week. I have to admit that I'm very tempted to call him."

I started to hand it back and she said, "Please, throw it away. I don't want that temptation."

"You have it memorized, right?"

"Yes," she said shyly.

"You won't get rid of that temptation by throwing away this match book," I said, "There are bigger issues here."

"I know," she said.

I explained what she already knew, she had panicked at reaching middle age and she had become hungry for compliments. "The attention of a younger man is very exciting. But have you given in?"

"Well, no, not yet"

"So what does your husband know about these evening adventures of yours?" I asked.

"He doesn't like it. But he doesn't know how far it almost went. Miles trusts me and I don't want to disappoint him."

Then she reversed that train of thought: "But I have never felt so alive as I have lately. I haven't felt this way since high school. And after all of those years of being a good wife and mother I feel like I deserve a little fun and excitement. You know, I might never get another chance."

"If you follow through with that line of thinking do you think he will forgive you?" I asked.

"Oh, I think he will forgive me because he is a very kind guy."

"And you are prepared to take advantage of him, right? Won't you feel guilty?"

"I didn't think of it that way. I guess I will deal with the guilt when it comes."

"I think you should think of your husband and your children. Why don't you try to put some excitement into your marriage."

"Miles is about as dull as he is kind. He's a nice guy but he is dull, dull, dull. His idea of a good time is to plop in front of the TV and begin to snore. I'm alive and I'm not going to let life pass me by while I sit and get fat again watching him snoozing in his recliner."

"You know how to have fun, so why not teach him?"

"He'd never want to. He likes his routine. I take care of the house, he works and goes to all his business meetings. Everything is just fine in his world. I don't think he ever knew how to have fun, even when he was a kid. His whole family are workaholics."

I insisted that Robin bring Miles in for the next session and we would work on making this marriage more enjoyable for everyone. I also got her promise that she would curtail her dangerous adventures from this point on as long as we were working on the marriage.

Regardless of what Robin said, I knew she wanted to make her marriage work. She would not have sought counseling if she was sure that she wanted to have an affair. She had a conflict about the allure of her adventures and her self-image as a good wife and mother.

Miles was a tall husky man with a quiet demeanor. My hand all but disappeared in his as he shook it. His calluses told a story of a lifetime of hard work.

The couple's session is summarized here.

Miles told me that he loved his wife very much and that her evening disappearances made him "nervous." He said that he had not confronted her about it because he felt it might "put her off even more." He thought she would get it out of her system and things would get back to normal.

"You say you love Robin, but tell me, Miles, how do you show it?" I asked.

"I think she knows that I love her. I never beat her and I don't drink or run around on her. I provide her with everything she wants."

"Is that enough, Robin?" I asked her.

"I know he loves me, but he doesn't say that very often. Yes, he gives me anything I want and we have never hurt for anything but I would like something more."

"What's that?" I asked.

"Fun, I want fun," she said.

At this, Miles seemed shocked. "Fun?" he asked.

"Yes, I want to have some fun. We just sit around. TV isn't fun, housework isn't fun, family get-togethers aren't fun. Playing solitaire until bed time isn't fun. I want to go places and do things. I want to feel like I'm important enough for you to take me out once in a while?"

Miles stared open-mouthed first at her and then at me as if to say he didn't understand.

"Well, Miles, how do you respond to that?" I asked.

"I didn't know she was thinking that way. I don't know what to say."

Robin looked at me, shrugged her shoulders and rolled her eyes.

The nice thing about Miles was that he was that he was willing to face the fact that his wife was not happy with their life. He did not accuse her of anything except not telling him how she felt. Once he understood her point of view he made some suggestions about things they could do together. They settled on taking lessons in Texas Line Dancing. That made Robin happy and she ended her adventures.

There was one complaint from Robin after that. She told me that other women were beginning to flirt with Miles at the dances. I smiled at her and she smiled back. She concluded that, as she said, "I guess it's true. What goes around comes around."

Comments

Robin had married Miles because he made her feel secure. He wasn't like the guys she had dated in high school. She felt she did not have to worry about him doing things to make her insecure. Unfortunately, the very thing that attracted her was the thing that irritated her later. This is often the case.

Miles made the assumption that is all too common with males that as long as they provide for their spouses and family their love can be assumed.

Robin thought Miles should know that she was unhappy without her telling him. She assumed that he did not want to make any changes and he assumed that she accepted things the way they were. Spouses need to be more expressive of their desires and feelings. Assumptions cause trouble.

Finally, marriage is not a low-maintenance concern. All spouses should keep this in mind and never forget it.

Steve and Ruth
Religious Domination

Steve had phoned in before they came. He wanted to be sure that the counselor would not violate their religious values. I told him that I did not think that would be a problem.

At the first session, Steve, a thin man of 55, wanted to let me know about their religion. They belonged to a small local church that has no affiliation with any other denomination. Steve and his brother, Bob, were the leaders of their growing congregation. Their parents had been the founding members and they retired and passed the mantel onto their sons.

Steve said that they take the Bible literally and their church is the only one that can truly call itself "Bible-based." He stopped here and asked if I believed in the Bible. I told him that I would prefer to leave my religious values out of the counseling and I would try to respect his whether they are similar or different. Counselors have an ethical commitment not to engage in religious discussions with their clients.

Steve added that he wanted to be sure that his religion would be respected and above all, he wanted to be sure that there would be confidentiality. He was a bit ashamed of seeking "worldly help" for their problems.

I asked Steve and Ruth to explain what they wanted to achieve by coming to counseling.

"I'll let Ruth explain it to you. She is the one who insists we get counseling."

Ruth was a plump woman around 30 years of age with short brown hair and glasses. She was wore a plain dress and sensible shoes. When she spoke, it was in a quiet voice a little high pitched.

"I don't think we are getting along very well. I don't feel very happy in our marriage. I have tried to be a good wife and a mother (they had three girls) but I just don't feel content. I don't know what's wrong!"

"Cast thy care upon the Lord and he shall sustain thee," Steve said.

Ruth rolled her eyes and said, "That doesn't help."

Steve looked crushed and said, "I wish her faith was stronger."

"I don't want to leave this marriage," Ruth continued, speaking to me, "but sometimes I feel trapped and I just want to run away!"

"Forsake not..." Steve began.

"Oh, shut up!" Ruth screamed.

Steve and I were both shocked at this. Ruth also looked a little surprised at herself. "I'm sorry, I shouldn't have done that," she apologized.

Before anything else could be said, I told Steve and Ruth—but mostly Steve—"Ruth has a great deal of stress and that stress just broke out from under the lid she had been trying to keep on it. Steve may not understand it and I don't understand it, but it is real. We have to respect that, don't you agree, Steve?"

Steve shook his head.

And we did. It took several sessions to get this couple back on track. I could measure progress by the decreasing frequency of Steve's use of Bible quotes in our sessions. As I pointed out to him, "Steve, it isn't the Bible that I have any argument with, it is the fact that you keep it between you and your wife."

Steve was a dominant and controlling husband and father. Once he understood that he actually began to make changes in his own way of relating.

I have to give Steve a lot of credit because it is not easy for a religious person to take a critical look at their own expression of that religion. Steve did not lose anything by putting the Bible down and relating to his wife as a person. The self-righteousness that goes along with religious leadership has been an object of ridicule and criticism for many years. It is more than a cliché, it is a temptation that is very hard to resist.

Not all my cases involving very religious people have gone as well as this one. I have been accused of doing the devil's work and bringing my clients down to the abyss by angry religious types who have not found me on their side. I have seen wife beaters and sex offenders refuse treatment because they have been "saved." I have also seen them justify their behavior by finding the right chapter and verse that they are able to twist to confirm their self-righteousness.

I have no quarrel with most religion but I do have a quarrel with using anything to dominate another person.

What happened with Steve and Ruth? As we got the Bible-quote barrier out of the way, we could deal with Steve's need to control and feel superior. We also had to deal with Ruth's depression. Although Steve did not like it, Ruth got a part-time job as a florist's assistant and found she was quite good at flower arranging. Steve had to accept this when he saw how good it was for her moods.

There were a few other details to work out but the in the final analysis, things worked out well for them.

Dwight and Marjorie
Motivation

When I went to the waiting room to get Dwight and Marjorie they were sitting as far as possible from each other. It was as if they did not want to be seen as a couple.

In my office, their postures continued to show antagonism toward each other. I began by introducing myself and told them how we would work together. Then I asked them to tell me about their problems from each point of view.

Silence.

I waited for a few seconds and then asked Marjorie to give me her point of view.

"He can tell you," she said and then folded her arms and stared at Dwight.

"He asked you," Dwight snapped and stared away from her.

"See," Marjorie said as she turned to me, "He is totally unresponsive. He won't talk about anything. I never know what he feels or what he thinks until he gets mad. Then he just stomps out of the house."

Dwight exhaled audibly.

The first session went on like that. The hostility was thick in the air and each bit of information had to be extracted like teeth from these people. I learned that communication had broken down (obviously) and they could no long discuss anything without arguing. Dwight often used his tactic of just leaving the situation when things got hot. Neither could tell me of any thing that they enjoyed together. In fact, neither one had a positive thing to say about their marriage or the other party.

I asked them about motivation. They reluctantly admitted that they wanted to be happy together "for the children's sake." I told them that staying together for the sake of the children was another way of saying they were torturing the children for the sake of their marital battles. I told them that children are a good reason for trying to make the marriage work but an unhappy marriage is no good for anyone.

Finally, I assigned them to spend an hour together in the week before the next appointment. I told them that they each had to try to make it a pleasant experience for the other.

The next week I was happy to see that they returned. After we had settled in my office I asked, "Well, how did it go?"

"What?" Marjorie asked.

"I had prescribed an hour together. How did it go?"

"We didn't do it. He didn't seem interested so I didn't see any point in it."

"What about you, Dwight?" I asked.

"Oh, I was interested but since she didn't bring it up, I would have felt like a fool begging her for a date."

"Well, let me ask you a question," I began, "Are you each motivated to make this marriage work?"

Silence

"Dwight, on a scale of 1 to 10 how would you rate your motivation to make this marriage work?" I asked.

"Depends," Dwight answered.

"Depends on what?" I asked.

"Depends on how much she wants it."

It is obvious by now that this couple has a relationship that has deteriorated from positive to negative. Couple relationships start out as positive/positive. In other words, in the beginning each one presented positive strokes in response to the other's positive strokes. As time went on, they shifted to negative/negative. For this to happen occasionally isn't unusual or even pathological. What is pathological is when they get stuck there, as Dwight and Marjorie did.

In the negative/negative relationship, each one is afraid to let his or her guard down. They have experienced that in the past. One offer a positive to the other and the other would counter with a negative. This couple provided an example:

Dwight, on coming home from work one day Dwight came up to Marjorie and said, "My, don't you look nice today!"

Marjorie "What the hell do you want?"

Dwight retreated into silence. That hurt.

On another occasion, Marjorie got up early and was making herself a sandwich for work. She decided to make one for Dwight to take for his lunch. She put it in his lunch bag and left it on the kitchen counter. When he came to the kitchen, Dwight looked in his bag and took the sandwich out, laid it on the counter and began to make his own.

That also hurt.

Dwight retreated from Marjorie because he did not want to be hurt. In a later session he revealed that he hated to speak up because she criticized almost everything he said. Marjorie, too, disclosed that he did and said things that hurt her feelings. The positive interactions had almost totally ceased and their usual interaction was negative/negative.

The negative/negative interaction creates suspicion as well as antagonism. She couldn't trust his compliments and he couldn't accept her sandwich. When the negativism dominates, neither party wants to accept that the other one could be nice. To accept that the other one has a nice side would make it difficult to remain hostile. If you accept that your adversary can be nice to you, you might let your guard down and that might lead to being hurt again. Besides that, you probably still feel like you have a lot of getting even to do.

When I asked them to rate their motivation, neither could do it because that would involve letting their guards down in front of the other. If he had said he rated his motivation for making the marriage work at a 10, he was afraid she would have attacked the sincerity of that remark. If she didn't she would probably rate her motivation at a much lower number in order to show him that he had to convince her that she should value the relationship more.

This situation illustrates why the couple needs to have a third party involved. They were at an impasse and neither could easily break through it without help. I did see them individually and found that both had high motivation to make the marriage work. They also had a lot of wounds from their negative/negative interactions.

I continued to insist that they have a positive hour and this time they did. Actually, they had to do it three times before it was a truly enjoyable experience. Then the relationship turned around and they began to build a positive relationship. The "date" gave each an opportunity to break the negative cycle and once that was broken the effects began to spread throughout their other interactions.

A negative/negative relationship is still a relationship and as long as there is some sort of relationship, there is hope.

Beth
Forming and Nourishing Attitudes

Beth was keeping her eyes on the road. It was a long, boring commute. Ellen, Darla and Claire were fighting the boredom by talking about their favorite subject, men.

"Ross won't let go of that remote to save his soul," Darla said, "One day he couldn't find it and you'd think he was having a heart attack."

"You know what a remote unit is, don't you?" Claire chimed in, "It's his penis. Good god, do they love their units!"

Everyone laughed.

"It's that old control thing. Men have to be in charge," Ellen said.

"I'm still thinking about what Claire said," Darla laughed, "the whole symbolism needs to be exploring."

"Yeah, I think there is something about all that channel flipping we should examine," Claire said. Maybe they just can't settle on one channel and commit themselves to it."

"That's it!" Ellen said, "Their units lead them from one channel to another."

"And their eyes flip from one woman to another," Darla added.

"Boy, ain't that the truth! Mark just can't keep his eyes off other women," Ellen said. "I can't stand going anywhere with him especially during the summer. I'm amazed his eyes stay in his head."

"Al could get whip lash with those double-takes he did at the mall last week, " Darla said, "God, it's embarrassing! I feel like turning invisible when he does that."

"Last month I went for a walk at lunch time and got hooted by a couple of cab drivers," Ellen said.

"Men are so stupid. Do they actually think that women like that kind of crap?" Claire said, "Do they think it turns us on or something?"

"I don't know what they're thinking—or if." Darla said.

"Oh, it isn't so hard to figure out what they're thinking. We're back to those remote units again. That explains the whole thing," Claire said.

"Get this, gals, "Darla said. " The other day I was talking to Jan Michaels on the phone. We were talking about her medical problems. She said that her doctor told her that it might be uterine cancer. He wants to do a biopsy. Jan's upset about it and I was just trying to be a friend.

"Then Al walked in. 'Who you talking to?" he asked. I mouthed 'Jan' and he shouted 'Oooh, sexy Jan!' and did that thing with his tongue. You know what I mean?

"Jan just said she'd call back later and hung up. I told Al that it had been a serious conversation and all he could think of saying was that he thought Jan was the sexiest woman he ever saw, and "I didn't mean anything by it.'"

"The jerk!" Ellen said.

"Yeah, the jerk. He wasn't sensitive to your feelings or to Jan's," Claire said.

"Ross has never been quite that jerkie," Darla said, "but I do wish he could just hug me without starting to drag me off to the bed room. It gets so I'm afraid to be affectionate with him."

"I know what you mean," Ellen said, "I can't even give him a kiss anymore unless I want to spend the next two hours in self-defense mode."

"Jerks and pigs!" Darla said.

"Jerks and pigs!" The three echoed in unison.

"Beth, you're being awfully quiet. Do you have anything to add? Let's hear a little biting humor from the captain of this ship," Ellen said.

"I don't have anything to add."

"Come on, Beth, don't tell us Joe is the perfect man." Ellen added.

"Not perfect but I think we have a good thing going."

"Oh, get off it. We just want to have a little fun ragging on the jerks," Darla said.

"Yeah, we're just passing time," Claire said.

"Well, I know that men can be jerks, but so can women," Beth said. "But I don't think it helps our attitudes any to keep ragging on them. You all know that I used to do that as much as anybody, but I started noticing that I was carrying that mentality into my relationship with Joe and it was bringing both of us down.

"Whenever I saw something I didn't like I made him aware of it. I found out that he was just not aware of a lot of it. I was the same. He got so he would make me aware of some things that bugged him. He made some changes and so have I."

"Beth, you're throwing a wet blanket on this whole thing. We are just trying to pass the time. It's all in fun," Ellen said.

"I just think it is a mistake to for me because of what it does to my attitude. I know what's good for me and that's all I can say. I find it's best if I respect Joe whether he is with me or not," Beth said.

Comment

In the evolution of a relationship, there is a phase where complaining about the opposite sex seems to be the fashion. Beth had passed through that phase and she and her partner had evidently passed through that phase and had entered a more mature level.

Beth and her husband had made a conscious effort to move into that phase. They were sensitive enough to know that disrespecting one another with friends hurt their attitudes toward one another.

I met another woman who had made that transition. She had been in a battered women's group offered by a local church. It had no leader and the members decided that the best way to deal with their problems was to complain about their partners. Meg wanted to restore her marriage of twenty years, not tear it down so she came for counseling. Eventually, she and her husband got back together. They both learned how to respect each other.

Psychologically, behavior changes from the inside out and the outside in. How we talk influences how we feel. How we feel influences how we act. Soon the fun of "spouse bashing" turns into something more serious than just friends playing put-down games.

If you want to make your relationship work, you have to build that respect for your partner in your words and deeds.

Howie's Choice

"Squit!" Ted yelled and punctuated this contraction of "Let's quit!" with a shrill whistle as he pointed to his watch.

"It's Miller time!" Mike said to the obvious approval of the rest of the crew.

"The hotter it is the better the beer!" Steve said.

"Howie, are you coming?" Bob asked.

"Oh, I don't know. I should get home."

"Wife got your jewels? Todd said. "Come on, one beer won't kill you. You can make up later."

Howie put his drill back in the toolbox and snapped the lock shut. He wiped his hands on a rag in the back of his pickup and went to the cab. "I guess one won't hurt," he said.

"Well, Hall-lay-looo-yah!" Mike shouted from his car, "The man's got balls!" As usual, he got a big laugh from his buddies.

"Mandie's not going to like that," Ted said, sticking his head in Howie's pickup window.

"I know," Howie said, "but a beer might taste good right now. It has been a hot one."

"Howie, how long have you and Mandie been married?"

"A little over a year."

"How's it going?"

Howie pulled his key out of the ignition and turned to Ted. "What are you, my boss during the day and my marriage counselor after the whistle blows?"

"Hey, man, I'm just a guy who's been over the road a few times. I don't like to see guys making mistakes like I did. I just want you to stop and think about what you're doing."

"Ted, I have thought about it. I want to have a beer with the guys and I don't think there's anything wrong with that."

"Nothing at all," Ted said, "but it looks to me that you are doing that just because the other guys would get on your case if you didn't. Isn't that right?"

"I think it is important to have a beer with your buddies every now and then. Even you do that. I'll just have one beer and head for home."

"Howie, you know if you try to leave after one beer you'll get the same razzing that they always give you. One won't do it. Two won't do it. Next thing you know…."

"Ok, I get your meaning. Still, I don't like them thinking I'm some kind of wuss or something."

"Look, Howie, nothing's going to change those guys. Their priority is to have a good time and they live up to that pretty well. I think you have other priorities, don't you?"

"What do you mean?"

"I mean that you are married. You aren't the kind of guy to throw that all away. Am I right?"

"Sure, but…"

"I don't want to preach to you, Howie, but you should know what the most important things in your life are and don't let anything get in the way of your pursuit of them. It's OK to have fun and all that but you shouldn't let that destroy your goals and priorities."

"You know, Ted, I never thought about goals and priorities very much. I didn't think I had any."

"Just because you never spelled them out doesn't mean they weren't there. You can tell what a person's goals and priorities are by looking at what they do—how they spend their time and their money. Those are good guys but their marriages just aren't number one any more. That's why Mike is going through a divorce and why I went through one, myself."

"You were divorced? I didn't know that. What happened?"

"Now, you're the counselor, right?" Ted laughed.

"Just curious," Howie said.

"What happened?" Ted continued. "I found out a basic lesson the hard way. I found out that marriage is not a low-maintenance deal. I just got married and continued living my life like I had before. After a couple of years I found out Carol was filing for a divorce. I didn't realize things were that bad. I knew we had some rough spots but I thought everyone went through what we were going through.

"I got the papers while I was at work. I was shocked. I quit early and called Carol and asked her if we could talk. She said that she had asked me to talk before and I just blew it off. It was too late. I can still remember pleading with her to go to counseling but she reminded me that I had laughed at that suggestion just a month before. She told me that she had made up her mind and I had better not call her again.

"I moved out like she asked. I went to counseling. Carol didn't. She went ahead with the divorce. You know what, Howie?"

"What?"

"You're looking at a sadder but wiser guy. If I can say something to some other guy that will save him the pain and expense of making the mistakes I made, I'll speak up.

"So, I've said my piece. I've stuck my nose into your private life as far as I intend. I am giving you the benefit of the education I paid dearly for and I'm giving it to you free. Make your marriage a top priority and don't treat it like it's a low-maintenance deal. I've said my piece, you do what you want. See you tomorrow."

With that, Ted walked to his pick-up. Howie turned the key and his engine turned over. He put it in gear and drove to the street. Ted watched to see if he would follow the other men to the left. Howie turned right.

Comments

Peer pressure does not end when you leave school. It still takes courage to go against it. Howie had the help of a good friend who had the guts to interfere in his personal business.

As Howie said, there is nothing wrong with having a beer with your friends, but when it takes away from the relationship, it is the wrong choice. Howie might arrange with his wife that he will do that one day, but when she is expecting him home, it is wrong to frustrate her expectations.

The cost of letting your priorities slip can be very high, indeed. It can be a cost in money as well as the personal cost that comes at failing in a relationship. We all have to make Howie's choice and decide in favor of our relationship.

Epilogue

PLAYING GOTCHA

We all grow up in a "gotcha!" world. Our parents watched for our little misbehaviors when we were toddlers. Our teachers looked for our misbehaviors in the school. Then the police are there with their "gotcha" lights on top of their cars. Gotcha, gotcha, gotcha!!!

We need a revolution. We need to change everything around. We need to play "gotcha" with good behavior. We need to reward people for being good and not for being bad. And we might as well start that with our children.

Why should we do that? One reason: it makes people feel good about themselves. Isn't it nicer to give out compliments than to give out criticism. In addition, unless you are too weird, it feels better to get attention for good behavior than the kind you receive for bad.

There is a simple rule about relationships. It is so simple that when I tell you about it you will think I am not telling you something new. I am pointing out the obvious; but sometimes the obvious is neglected. Are you ready? Are you sure you are ready? Ok, then, here it is:

What you pay attention to you will get more of.

If you pay attention to a child's tantrums, you will find the number increasing. If you pay attention to a teen's mistakes you will probably find more mistakes being made. If you pay attention to a spouse's poor table manners, you may just get more of them.

On the other hand, if you praise the child for sharing her toys she will begin to value sharing. If you notice that the teen has made fewer mistakes in math you are encouraging to that child. Moreover, if you let your spouse know that you appreciate the littlest things then you will cement your relationship and encourage the continued behavior of a similar nature.

Moreover, if you give goodies you feel good. Moreover, the attention goodies are very inexpensive but very dear. Even the poorest peasant can give attention and notice the behavior they want to see increased.

A few years ago some enterprising teachers taught some mentally handicapped children to praise the "normal" children with whom they shared a playground. They were taught to say thank you to any of them that played ball with them or did anything at all nice. The result was that handicapped children were welcomed into some of the playground activities and sometimes even helped with their studies by the children who used to tease them. In addition, best of all (no surprise) everyone felt good!

It does not always have to be praise. Sometimes it is just a case of noticing. People love feedback about their behavior—if it is positive. Moreover, people can take some of the bitter feedback better with some of the sweet.

If you want to play positive "gotcha" you have to learn to identify the behaviors you are looking for and find the best way to pay attention to them.

Behavior is observable: "being a good little boy" is not a behavior, it's a value judgment on the part of the adult. Sharing toys is more like it, "behaving yourself" is not. "Playing nice" is a little vague but picking up the toys and putting them in the toy box is better.

You cannot reward abstractions, attitudes, moods or ideas. You need to be specific. You might use statements that start out with "when." "When you compliment my cooking, I feel really important." Or, "When you come home right after work, I feel like you do care about me."

And after you have played positive "Gotcha" for a while you'll find that others pick it up. And when others pick it up it becomes a fad among a few and before you know it, it grows into a trend in the community and finally it becomes a real movement and in the end it will take over the world.

Now wouldn't that be nice?

Does it work?

This is the final chapter of the book. I keep thinking of things I want to add to it because I want your relationship to be a success. I finally decided to end it this book with the most basic point that you should ask yourself in achieving any important goal. I firmly believe that marriage is one of the most character-building adventures any person can set out to accomplish. I want you to take this chapter very seriously. The point is never about the theory or the personality of a counselor it is about that basic question, "Does it work."

I'm sure you have probably heard the joke about the guy who is wandering around under a street light late at night when a police officer comes up to him. "What are you doing?" the officer asks.

"Looking for my keys," the man replies without looking up.

The officer decides to help and turns his flashlight on and they both look for a while. Finally, he says to the man, "I don't think they are here. Are you sure this is where you lost them?"

"No, I lost them across the street, but the light is better here."

Corny joke? Yep. I have another one.

The man sitting in the psychiatrist's office kept snapping his fingers and looking around the office.

"Tell me, sir why do you snap your fingers like that?" the psychiatrist asked.

"Keeps the elephants away."

"But there are no elephants near here…" the psychiatrist continued.

"Works!" replied the patient.

Insanity

You have probably heard this saying, "the definition of insanity is doing the same thing over again and hoping for different results." While mental health professionals would argue with this definition, it certainly defines one of the biggest forms of stupidity practiced by couples as they destroy their relationships.

Joe and Marcie could jump right into their act with the ease and facility of a pair of synchronized swimmers. They had the same pattern, which I will try to summarize for you.

Joe would accuse Marcie of screwing up the checkbook.

Marcie would deny it saying it was Joe's fault for not recording a check.

Joe would deny it and say he told her about it and she could have entered it.

Marcie would say he could enter it just as easily as she could.

Joe would remind her that she claimed she could handle the checking better than he could and that was obviously wrong.

Marcie would argue that no one could keep a checkbook straight if her husband was a spendthrift who did not enter his purchases.

Joe reacted to the word, "spendthrift," and reminded Marcie that she was the one who bought that set of earrings from the Home Shopping Network.

Marcie countered with his purchasing tools he never used.

You know how it goes. They eventually got around to bringing up previous flirtations with others, Joe's bout of gambling five years ago and Marcie's car accident two days after they got the new car (also five years ago). I don't know how they ended this ritual at home but I ended it in my office by telling them to "SHUT UP!!"

Because they seemed to enjoy this ritual, I let them repeat it one more time. Then I asked them if they felt at all stupid. They stared at me in shocked disbelief. They obviously did not expect a counselor to be so mean and insulting.

Well, it is true, isn't it? Repetition of this hurtful ritual may not be insane, but it certainly is stupid. Once I recapped their argument (this took a while because the old ritual kept rearing its ugly head), along with analysis they began to get it.

Marcie and Joe could see that they had been too involved in their own defenses to stand back and look at what they were doing. Eventually, as the light came through the clouds, they could even see that the one thing they were cooperating on was the destruction of their relationship.

Take a long hard look

Do yourself a favor and go sit on a hill far from all noise and distractions some early morning and while the sun is coming up, examine your behavior. Examine how you have interacted with your partner and ask yourself this question, "Is this working?"

Is the way you interact with your partner helping to bring you and your partner closer together or is it doing the opposite? That is simple, isn't it? Well, yes and no. It is a simple question but it is hard to remember to ask yourself that. That is why you need to go up on that hill in the quiet every now and then. Whether it is a hill, a bathtub, a front porch or patio, it does not matter. You need to have a place and time when you can ask that simple question.

A guy I will call, Ralph, came to me because his wife had told him that she was tired of trying to live with him. When he asked her to explain she said he should figure it out. Ralph could not figure it out by himself so he asked for help. After a little question and answer session, we figured out that he had been demanding, critical and cold toward her throughout their marriage.

Ralph had all the defenses you would expect but he was motivated to get beyond them in order to save his marriage. I gave him the "go up on a hill" formula and told him to think of it this way: "Think of a piece of paper with a line down the middle. On the right put down the things that you do that work toward your goal and on the left put down the things that don't." I took a piece of paper and illustrated what I meant. We wrote some examples from the past.

It was so simple that I was surprised at the look on his face. It looked like he had just met God. He took the paper and said he was going to take this with him. He told me he in the next session that he put it on his bathroom mirror.

It worked for Ralph. He had the right motivation and this simple concept worked for him. I had not intended him to do more than just keep the image in his mind but the visual image on that paper did the trick for him.

For you, I re-invite you to go up that hill all alone and ask yourself this simple question: "Does it work?"

A blessing:

> *May your hard times strengthen you,.*
> *May your happy times comfort you,,*
> *May your relationship be the envy of all,*
> *And may you frequently be absolutely*
> *giddy about each other.*

About the Author

Biography

Harold Renshaw got his formal education from several colleges, including Immaculate Conception Seminary College and the University of Missouri. He earned a Master's Degree from the latter.

He taught elementary school, worked in welfare and child protective services in Iowa before he ventured into working with families and couples. He has been a therapist, a supervisor, an agency administrator and college teacher.

Harold is happily married to a Betty and is grateful to her for her patient teaching even when she doesn't know she's doing it.

He has written a book for workers in residential treatment facilities, *Caring for Kids* (Reasearch Associates, 1981), *Precision Parenting* (self-published, 1972), *Taming Your Inner Jackass*, a book on anger management (Great Unpublished, 2000.)

0-595-22793-7

www.ingramcontent.com/pod-product-compliance
Lightning Source LLC
Chambersburg PA
CBHW061246280526
45784CB00002B/662